파고다토익 시험 직전 마무리 모의고사

해설 바로 보기

음원 바로 듣기

PAGODA Books

시험 진행 안내

❶ 시험 시간: 120분(2시간)
- Listening Comprehension 100문제: 45분
- Reading Comprehension 100문제: 75분
- L/C 진행 후 휴식 시간 없이 바로 R/C 진행

❷ 준비물
- 컴퓨터용 사인펜 또는 연필

❸ 시험 응시 준수 사항
- 시험 시작 10분 전 입실 (이후에는 입실 불가)
- 종료 30분 전과 10분 전에 시험 종료 공지함
- 휴대전화의 전원을 꺼둘 것

❹ OMR 답안지 표기 요령
- 반드시 컴퓨터용 사인펜 또는 연필로 표기
- 개인정보, 문제번호, 단체명, 문제번호, 학과(부서) 및 학번코드 표기
  (학과(부서)코드는 별도 공지)

※ 개인정보, 문제번호, 학과(부서)코드, 주민등록번호를 틀리게 표기했을 경우 채점 및 성적 확인이 불가능하므로 주의하시기 바랍니다.

답안 작성 요령 Sample
○   ● Ⓑ Ⓒ Ⓓ
×   Ⓐ Ⓑ ⊗ Ⓓ
×   Ⓐ Ⓑ Ⓒ Ⓓ
×   Ⓐ Ⓑ Ⓒ Ⓓ
×   Ⓐ Ⓑ Ⓒ Ⓓ

LISTENING TEST

In the Listening test, you will be asked to demonstrate how well you understand spoken English. The entire listening test will last approximately 45 minutes. There are four parts, and directions are given for each part. You must mark your answers on the separate answer sheet. Do not write your answers in your test book.

PART 1

Directions: For each question in this part, you will hear four statements about a picture in your test book. When you hear the statements, you must select the one statement that best describes what you see in the picture. Then find the number of the question on your answer sheet and mark your answer. The statements will not be printed in your test book and will be spoken only one time.

Statement (B), "A man is pointing at a document," is the best description of the picture, so you should select answer (B) and mark it on your answer sheet.

1.

2.

GO ON TO THE NEXT PAGE

3.

4.

5.

6.

PART 2

Directions: You will hear a question or statement and three responses spoken in English. They will not be printed in your test book and will be spoken only one time. Select the best response to the question or statement and mark the letter (A), (B), or (C) on your answer sheet.

7. Mark your answer on your answer sheet.
8. Mark your answer on your answer sheet.
9. Mark your answer on your answer sheet.
10. Mark your answer on your answer sheet.
11. Mark your answer on your answer sheet.
12. Mark your answer on your answer sheet.
13. Mark your answer on your answer sheet.
14. Mark your answer on your answer sheet.
15. Mark your answer on your answer sheet.
16. Mark your answer on your answer sheet.
17. Mark your answer on your answer sheet.
18. Mark your answer on your answer sheet.
19. Mark your answer on your answer sheet.
20. Mark your answer on your answer sheet.
21. Mark your answer on your answer sheet.
22. Mark your answer on your answer sheet.
23. Mark your answer on your answer sheet.
24. Mark your answer on your answer sheet.
25. Mark your answer on your answer sheet.
26. Mark your answer on your answer sheet.
27. Mark your answer on your answer sheet.
28. Mark your answer on your answer sheet.
29. Mark your answer on your answer sheet.
30. Mark your answer on your answer sheet.
31. Mark your answer on your answer sheet.

PART 3

Directions: You will hear some conversations between two or more people. You will be asked to answer three questions about what the speakers say in each conversation. Select the best response to each question and mark the letter (A), (B), (C), or (D) on your answer sheet. The conversations will not be printed in your test book and will be spoken only one time.

32. Where does the woman most likely work?

    (A) At a shipping company
    (B) At a marketing firm
    (C) At a farm
    (D) At a restaurant

33. What is the woman concerned about?

    (A) The quality of a brand
    (B) The date of a delivery
    (C) A decline in customers
    (D) An increase in prices

34. What does the woman decide to do?

    (A) Order a new product
    (B) Look at a catalog
    (C) Call a customer
    (D) Search for other suppliers

35. What are the speakers mainly discussing?

    (A) An office renovation
    (B) An annual conference
    (C) A training session
    (D) A corporate merger

36. According to the man, what will happen?

    (A) More stores will open.
    (B) New executives will be hired.
    (C) Employees will be relocated.
    (D) Overseas sales will increase.

37. What will take place next week?

    (A) A safety inspection
    (B) A contract signing
    (C) A grand opening
    (D) A staff meeting

38. Why is the woman going to Beijing?

    (A) To hire some workers
    (B) To purchase some electronics
    (C) To speak at a convention
    (D) To evaluate a production facility

39. What is the man worried about?

    (A) Meeting a deadline
    (B) Catching a flight
    (C) Finding qualified candidates
    (D) Improving working conditions

40. What does the man offer to do?

    (A) Provide feedback on a product
    (B) Give travel recommendations
    (C) Help out with a presentation
    (D) Conduct some interviews

41. Where is the conversation most likely taking place?

    (A) At a city library
    (B) At a television station
    (C) At an employment agency
    (D) At a publication company

42. What problem are the speakers discussing?

    (A) Some items are not available.
    (B) Some work needs to be revised.
    (C) A contract has not been submitted.
    (D) A program will not be broadcast.

43. What will the man do next?

    (A) Make an appointment
    (B) Contact an editor
    (C) Review an agreement
    (D) Repair a system

GO ON TO THE NEXT PAGE

44. Where are the speakers?

(A) At an electronics store
(B) At a car repair shop
(C) At an airport
(D) At a hotel

45. What problem does the woman mention?

(A) A business is short-staffed.
(B) An item is not in stock.
(C) A room is not available.
(D) A subway line is closed.

46. What will the man most likely do?

(A) Take a shuttle
(B) Ask for a refund
(C) Cancel a meeting
(D) Visit a Web site

47. What is the conversation mainly about?

(A) Changing a company policy
(B) Selecting a job candidate
(C) Handling customer complaints
(D) Purchasing new equipment

48. What does the woman propose?

(A) Working from home
(B) Demonstrating a product
(C) Promoting a current employee
(D) Organizing training sessions

49. What will the speakers probably do next?

(A) Give a presentation
(B) Review a procedure
(C) Interview some applicants
(D) Look at some documents

50. What did the woman do today?

(A) Spoke with a customer
(B) Delivered some packages
(C) Performed an inspection
(D) Ordered some equipment

51. Where does the conversation take place?

(A) At a movie theater
(B) At a train station
(C) At a shopping mall
(D) At a manufacturing plant

52. What does the woman suggest doing?

(A) Postponing a business trip
(B) Training an employee individually
(C) Introducing a special offer
(D) Changing a part immediately

53. Who most likely are the speakers?

(A) Maintenance workers
(B) Apartment tenants
(C) Real estate agents
(D) Property managers

54. What does the woman imply when she says, "the situation is different now"?

(A) Some workers are no longer needed.
(B) A task has been completed.
(C) Some equipment will be purchased.
(D) A decision should be reexamined.

55. What does the woman say she will do?

(A) Check some rooms
(B) Obtain some estimates
(C) Review a contract
(D) Post a notice

56. What does the man ask the woman to do?

(A) Manage a department
(B) Complete a report
(C) Attend a convention
(D) Train an employee

57. Why is the woman concerned?

(A) She cannot find some documents.
(B) She might arrive late to an event.
(C) She does not have enough time for a task.
(D) She has little knowledge about some products.

58. What does the man say he has already done?

(A) Reserved a room
(B) Submitted a report
(C) Visited other branches
(D) Prepared some notes

59. What industry does the man probably work in?

(A) Finance
(B) Corporate law
(C) Broadcasting
(D) Computer programming

60. What does the woman ask the man to do?

(A) Explain a product
(B) Return another day
(C) Sign some books
(D) Offer some advice

61. Why does the man say, "you can find out for yourself"?

(A) To advertise a seminar
(B) To encourage people to call a hotline
(C) To promote an online tool
(D) To invite listeners to enter a contest

DELIVERY SCHEDULE – AFTERNOON	
Kancane, Inc.	12:15 P.M.
Betatax Group	1:15 P.M.
Keyway Corporation	2:45 P.M.
Biotom Pharmaceuticals	3:45 P.M.

62. What kind of business do the speakers most likely work for?

(A) A clothing manufacturer
(B) A print shop
(C) A furniture store
(D) A catering company

63. Why did Ranlab Company call?

(A) To make a complaint
(B) To revise an order
(C) To ask for a discount
(D) To reschedule a meeting

64. Look at the graphic. When will Ranlab Company probably receive their delivery?

(A) At 12:15 P.M.
(B) At 1:15 P.M.
(C) At 2:45 P.M.
(D) At 3:45 P.M.

GO ON TO THE NEXT PAGE

Brennan Inn	
1st Floor	Lobby
2nd Floor	Restaurant
3rd Floor	Conference Rooms
4th Floor	Laundry Area
5th - 12th Floor	Guest Rooms

International Physicians Conference Fees		
Attending day 1 only	Association member	$115
	Non-member	$125
Attending day 2 only	Association member	$140
	Non-member	$155
Full attendance	Association member	$230
	Non-member	$250

65. What most likely is the man's occupation?

(A) Event coordinator
(B) Tour operator
(C) Restaurant manager
(D) Front desk receptionist

66. What does the woman want to do?

(A) Print some brochures
(B) Invite guests
(C) Wash some clothes
(D) Change rooms

67. Look at the graphic. Which floor will the woman go to next?

(A) The 1st floor
(B) The 2nd floor
(C) The 3rd floor
(D) The 4th floor

68. What problem is the man calling about?

(A) Some events have been canceled.
(B) A Web site cannot be accessed.
(C) Some equipment is not available.
(D) A speaker will arrive late.

69. Look at the graphic. How much will the man's conference fee be?

(A) $115
(B) $125
(C) $140
(D) $155

70. What information does the woman ask for?

(A) An e-mail address
(B) A venue location
(C) Some numbers on a card
(D) Some names on a list

PART 4

Directions: You will hear some talks given by a single speaker. You will be asked to answer three questions about what the speaker says in each talk. Select the best response to each question and mark the letter (A), (B), (C), or (D) on your answer sheet. The talks will not be printed in your test book and will be spoken only one time.

71. What service is the speaker advertising?

    (A) A business travel plan
    (B) A corporate relocation plan
    (C) A mobile phone plan
    (D) An office management plan

72. What does the speaker emphasize about the service?

    (A) It offers the lowest prices.
    (B) It is the easiest to use.
    (C) It has an unlimited warranty.
    (D) It can be used in other countries.

73. According to the speaker, what can be found on the Web site?

    (A) Customer reviews
    (B) Opening hours
    (C) A user manual
    (D) A payment schedule

74. Where does the caller work?

    (A) At a restaurant
    (B) At a staffing agency
    (C) At a doctor's office
    (D) At a museum

75. What is the purpose of the message?

    (A) To explain a building layout
    (B) To request a revised document
    (C) To book a company lunch
    (D) To offer an appointment time

76. What has recently changed?

    (A) The location of a business
    (B) The number of guests
    (C) An event schedule
    (D) A service charge

77. Why is the speaker calling?

    (A) To give a cost estimate
    (B) To check an appointment
    (C) To report a problem with a project
    (D) To explain details about a delivery

78. What does the speaker imply when he says, "you might want to reconsider this"?

    (A) A budget might need to be increased.
    (B) A location should be changed.
    (C) A deadline may be extended.
    (D) An additional worker could be required.

79. What will the speaker send to the listener?

    (A) A questionnaire
    (B) A brochure
    (C) A sales receipt
    (D) A revised plan

80. What does the speaker say will take place on the weekend?

    (A) A system upgrade
    (B) A company workshop
    (C) An office renovation
    (D) A management meeting

81. What are listeners asked to do?

    (A) Work additional hours
    (B) Prepare some training materials
    (C) Create a new password
    (D) Inform workers about a procedure

82. Who most likely is David Redmond?

    (A) An event organizer
    (B) An IT employee
    (C) An interior designer
    (D) An HR manager

GO ON TO THE NEXT PAGE

83. What does the speaker say is special about the zoo?

(A) It features natural environments.
(B) It gives membership discounts.
(C) It has high-tech facilities.
(D) It offers a wide variety of activities.

84. What are listeners encouraged to do at the end of the tour?

(A) Fill out a form
(B) Check a map
(C) Have a meal
(D) Look at a book

85. According to the speaker, what is NOT allowed during the tour?

(A) Giving food to animals
(B) Making calls with cell phones
(C) Taking pictures
(D) Hitting cages

86. Where do the listeners most likely work?

(A) At a music studio
(B) At an advertising firm
(C) At a car manufacturer
(D) At a film company

87. What does the speaker imply when she says, "I've never heard of such a thing"?

(A) She is not sure about a plan.
(B) She is unaware of a report.
(C) She is impressed by a result.
(D) She is interested in a product.

88. What does the speaker want to do in June?

(A) Meet with an actor
(B) Finish a recording
(C) Hold a workshop
(D) Produce a new vehicle

89. What does Quadcity, Inc. sell?

(A) Home appliances
(B) Fitness products
(C) Cleaning supplies
(D) Food supplements

90. What do people like about the new line of merchandise?

(A) It is made to last a long time.
(B) It is safe for the environment.
(C) It is sold at reasonable prices.
(D) It is available in different sizes.

91. What does the speaker say will happen in November?

(A) A marketing campaign will start.
(B) A new radio show will be broadcast.
(C) A store grand opening will be held.
(D) A national conference will take place.

92. What type of merchandise does the store carry?

(A) Office supplies
(B) Clothing
(C) Groceries
(D) Sports equipment

93. Why have some displays been rearranged?

(A) To create space for more customers
(B) To prepare for a safety inspection
(C) To make certain products more visible
(D) To hold an employee training session

94. What does the speaker imply when he says, "this is one of the busiest times of the year"?

(A) Some items will be sold at lowered prices.
(B) A delivery date is uncertain.
(C) The store will be open later than usual.
(D) More workers are needed.

Tour Schedule	
City Walk and Lunch	12:00 P.M.
Garden Visit	2:30 P.M.
Theater Show	5:30 P.M.
Dinner	7:00 P.M.

95. What does the speaker say about Augustine Diner?

    (A) It has hired a famous chef.
    (B) It has an outdoor dining area.
    (C) It was featured in a magazine.
    (D) It was established a long time ago.

96. Look at the graphic. What time is this talk most likely being given?

    (A) At 12:00 P.M.
    (B) At 2:30 P.M.
    (C) At 5:30 P.M.
    (D) At 7:00 P.M.

97. What will the speaker distribute to the listeners?

    (A) Some snacks
    (B) Audio equipment
    (C) Protective gloves
    (D) Information pamphlets

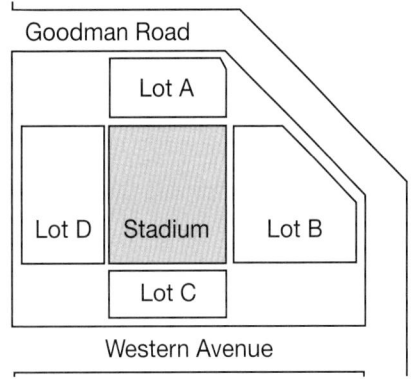

98. Why was the soccer game canceled?

    (A) The weather was poor.
    (B) Some equipment was missing.
    (C) The stadium needed repairs.
    (D) Some athletes were injured.

99. According to the speaker, why might a listener watch a game on television?

    (A) If there is heavy traffic
    (B) If the venue is changed
    (C) If the parking areas are full
    (D) If tickets are unavailable

100. Look at the graphic. Which parking lot will NOT be accessible?

    (A) Lot A
    (B) Lot B
    (C) Lot C
    (D) Lot D

This is the end of the Listening test. Turn to Part 5 in your test book.

GO ON TO THE NEXT PAGE

READING TEST

In the Reading test, you will read a variety of texts and answer several different types of reading comprehension questions. The entire Reading test will last 75 minutes. There are three parts, and directions are given for each part. You are encouraged to answer as many questions as possible within the time allowed.

You must mark your answers on the separate answer sheet. Do not write your answers in your test book.

PART 5

Directions: A word or phrase is missing in each of the sentences below. Four answer choices are given below each sentence. Select the best answer to complete the sentence. Then mark the letter (A), (B), (C), or (D) on your answer sheet.

101. ------- part-time employee at Carter Fitness Center is provided with regular training on new equipment.

(A) Every
(B) As
(C) Other
(D) Only

102. Mr. Jung couldn't be here today, but he ------- comes to all employee training sessions.

(A) poorly
(B) roughly
(C) usually
(D) formerly

103. Due to growing customer demand, it would be ------- to expand the product selection this quarter.

(A) senses
(B) sensibly
(C) sensible
(D) sensibility

104. Casual clothes are not considered ------- for the company's anniversary banquet.

(A) helpful
(B) appropriate
(C) meaningful
(D) important

105. From May 1, Human Resources will issue business expense reimbursements ------- by direct deposit.

(A) separately
(B) separation
(C) separates
(D) separating

106. Your responsibilities as a market researcher are essentially the same as -------.

(A) him
(B) he
(C) himself
(D) his

107. When obtaining employment visas, applicants have to provide ------- of graduation from their university.

(A) proof
(B) basis
(C) support
(D) draft

108. The proposed extension of subway line 5 to Castlerock will generate a ------- demand for construction workers.

(A) sizable
(B) correct
(C) fragile
(D) wealthy

109. The Chief Financial Officer suggested an initial threshold ------- $5,000 for international shipments.

(A) around
(B) onto
(C) of
(D) against

110. After just two months as department manager, Mr. Kim has attended ------- a dozen conferences.

(A) nearer
(B) near
(C) nearing
(D) nearly

111. Daniel Simone is one of the most successful science fiction authors in North America, ------- only Carlos Montoya in book sales.

(A) through
(B) past
(C) behind
(D) along

112. Park Consulting's headquarters is ------- relocating to Sydney next month with two new teams.

(A) dependably
(B) routinely
(C) formally
(D) incrementally

113. Since she assumed control of TRO, Inc. in March, Marina Dament has earned the ------- of her peers.

(A) respected
(B) respectful
(C) respect
(D) respects

114. ------- several celebrities have endorsed Hikem Sportswear in TV commercials, many people in the country prefer Gadira Athletic's products.

(A) Now that
(B) Wherever
(C) Although
(D) In fact

115. Tourism is the ------- income source for the majority of businesses in the Grande Cay area.

(A) certain
(B) primary
(C) initial
(D) inherent

116. Customers at Hawk's Gardening Store should ask an employee for help rather than trying to carry heavy items -------.

(A) their
(B) them
(C) their own
(D) themselves

117. Karen Swift, lead scientist at DF Labs, is the ------- of this year's Outstanding Research Award.

(A) recipient
(B) receive
(C) receivable
(D) receipt

118. Fremont Bank and Trust will be opening a third branch ------- next spring.

(A) anything
(B) everyone
(C) sometime
(D) whenever

119. Ms. Boumaza is ------- with launching several promotions that have greatly improved the company's profits.

(A) evaluated
(B) credited
(C) agreed
(D) believed

120. Leonidas Athletics will make a $3 million ------- in equipment to the World Sporting Association's charity, Sports for Kids.

(A) submission
(B) conservation
(C) donation
(D) possession

GO ON TO THE NEXT PAGE

121. Porto Petro is under growing ------- to increase its production capabilities.

    (A) control
    (B) pressure
    (C) awareness
    (D) guidance

122. The Royal Academy is highly respected ------- the Spanish-speaking world as an authority on the proper use of the language.

    (A) concerning
    (B) abroad
    (C) throughout
    (D) toward

123. The city's proposal ------- the historic courthouse on Rye Avenue will be open to public feedback next Thursday.

    (A) restoring
    (B) restore
    (C) to restore
    (D) restored

124. We ------- the specifications yesterday, but our engineering department said they needed more time.

    (A) can send
    (B) must have sent
    (C) would have sent
    (D) should send

125. ------- patient appointments is one of the medical office assistant's most important responsibilities.

    (A) Schedule
    (B) Scheduling
    (C) Scheduled
    (D) To schedule

126. Management predicts that the heavy snow will ------- the January operations of Geon Logistics.

    (A) reflect on
    (B) fall behind
    (C) result in
    (D) interfere with

127. Due to increased interest in the Art Expo, the early registration period to get discounted tickets -------.

    (A) to be extending
    (B) have extended
    (C) has been extended
    (D) extended

128. Lately, the university library has received a number of large donations, ------- are from former students.

    (A) considering that
    (B) the reason for
    (C) most of which
    (D) due to them

129. Bayers Equipment has ------- from a local retailer to an international sports brand in the last 10 years.

    (A) evolved
    (B) projected
    (C) gathered
    (D) ranged

130. To have an article included in our next issue, it must be received at least two weeks ------- the publication date.

    (A) forward
    (B) ahead of
    (C) almost
    (D) in spite of

PART 6

Directions: Read the texts that follow. A word, phrase, or sentence is missing in parts of each text. Four answer choices for each question are given below the text. Select the best answer to complete the text. Then mark the letter (A), (B), (C), or (D) on your answer sheet.

Questions 131-134 refer to the following e-mail.

From: Hyun-sung Kim, Staff Training Department
To: All staff
Subject: Workshop series
Date: August 30

Dear all,

The first of the company's professional development workshops will take place on September 12. This ------- workshop will be led by Brett Myers, author of the best-selling
131.
book, *Doing the Deal*. Mr. Myers ------- how participants can better negotiate with potential
132.
clients. This session will be the only one in the workshop series that will focus on negotiation skills. -------.
133.

If you or any of your staff would like to participate, please obtain ------- your direct
134.
supervisor and sign up by the end of this week.

Many thanks.

Hyun-sung Kim

---

131. (A) updated
(B) upcoming
(C) rescheduled
(D) last

132. (A) had explained
(B) explained
(C) will explain
(D) would have explained

133. (A) The rest will cover other subjects, such as project management and budgeting.
(B) Online training is gaining in popularity throughout the industry.
(C) When he was an employee here, Mr. Myers led several training courses.
(D) Many companies are publishing business books these days.

134. (A) who authorizes
(B) authorizing
(C) having authorized
(D) the authorization of

GO ON TO THE NEXT PAGE

Questions 135-138 refer to the following letter.

Tanuja Rajagopalan
Nimtincan Manufacturing
Lucknow 226031
Uttar Pradesh
India

Dear Ms. Rajagopalan,

We are writing to inform you that there may be some minor ------- for orders placed during
135.
the week of September 18. In order to improve our service to our customers, we are
relocating our main warehouse to a new facility. -------. We expect the move to take no more
136.
than eight days, ------- which time we anticipate shipping orders to take half a day longer
137.
than usual. ------- your orders are delivered on time, we recommend that you place your
138.
next order before September 11. We apologize in advance for any inconvenience this may

cause.

Sincerely,

Joseph Lin
Customer Relations Director

135. (A) delays
(B) additions
(C) exceptions
(D) charges

136. (A) Order tracking is provided for all customers at our Web site.
(B) Our supply of this item will be limited in availability.
(C) Warehouse rental is a competitive business in our area.
(D) This will give us storage space for many more products.

137. (A) less than
(B) because of
(C) upon
(D) during

138. (A) Ensure
(B) Ensured
(C) To ensure
(D) While ensuring

Questions 139-142 refer to the following article.

WTA Town Hall Meeting
November 21
By Lauren Bicker

The Westerpond Transit Authority (WTA) will be hosting a town hall meeting at the Ralf Herrick Community Center on Wednesday, November 29, at 6:30 P.M. The purpose of the meeting is to discuss a plan to double train service on major commuter rail lines. -------. Local residents have voiced concern that the extra trains will cause more noise and pollution. -------, the WTA is researching ways to reduce the environmental impact of the service expansion. At the town hall meeting, Edmund Emanuel from the WTA will go over what kinds of methods the residents can ------- to see used to minimize environmental damage. A ------- with Governor Stephanie Snell will follow.

139. (A) WTA meetings are held on the last Wednesday of every month.
(B) The WTA completed the project despite a limited budget.
(C) The new transportation director has extensive experience in a related field.
(D) These lines pass through several school zones.

140. (A) As a result
(B) As an example
(C) As expected
(D) As usual

141. (A) convince
(B) remember
(C) expect
(D) permit

142. (A) discuss
(B) discussing
(C) discussion
(D) will discuss

GO ON TO THE NEXT PAGE

Questions 143-146 refer to the following e-mail.

From: m.tiburcio@duophase.com
To: kalla@plexjob.com
Subject: Galliant products
Date: May 19

Dear Ms. Kalla,

I am a senior buyer at Duophase Stores. I am contacting you because we are interested in ------- our offerings to include products like your company's. We are considering selling waterproof backpacking boots in our outlets. Since this ------- requires a special type of nylon, we called the Fiber Manufacturers Association, who suggested checking with your company. Upon reviewing your catalog, we saw that you do ------- make what we are looking for. We would like to start with a small order. -------. Please advise your pricing policy for higher-volume customers.

I look forward to hearing your thoughts and discussing this further with you.

Sincerely,

Marcos Tiburcio
Duophase Stores

143. (A) diversifies
(B) diversify
(C) diversified
(D) diversifying

144. (A) model
(B) capability
(C) reply
(D) solution

145. (A) individually
(B) very
(C) indeed
(D) nonetheless

146. (A) Please visit our Web site to fill out a customer survey.
(B) We may, however, increase our order size later on.
(C) Regrettably, these will soon be out of stock due to increased demand.
(D) Our firm has been a member of this community for more than 50 years.

PART 7

Directions: In this part you will read a selection of texts, such as magazine and newspaper articles, e-mails, and instant messages. Each text or set of texts is followed by several questions. Select the best answer for each question and mark the letter (A), (B), (C), or (D) on your answer sheet.

Questions 147-148 refer to the following memo.

To: All Staff
From: Peter Allard
Subject: Laptops
Date: Monday, September 10

Tomorrow morning, new laptops will be given to all staff members who have requested them. Please remember that the machines may not be removed from the office building. Any employees who do so will lose their privileges to use company equipment. There will be a training session on Thursday to provide instruction on how to properly use the machines. Everyone who receives a laptop must attend this session. It will last from 9 A.M. to 11 A.M. Feel free to speak with me if you encounter any problems with your laptop.

147. What is suggested about the laptops?

(A) They will arrive on Thursday.
(B) They must be paid for by employees.
(C) They cannot be taken home.
(D) They can only be used by managers.

148. Why would a staff member contact Mr. Allard?

(A) To resolve an equipment problem
(B) To request a vacation day
(C) To participate in a survey
(D) To sign up for a convention

GO ON TO THE NEXT PAGE

Questions 149-150 refer to the following letter.

Michael Shumfield
3948 Berly Lane
Artesia, CA 90701

April 29

Dear Mr. Shumfield,

We at Natural Foods are pleased to inform you about an exciting opportunity. You are now eligible to become a member of our shoppers club. Membership will provide you with discounts every time you shop with us. You will also receive a coupon booklet each month. To apply for membership, fill out the enclosed form. You can return it to us by mail or give it to a manager the next time you shop at Natural Foods. Within a week, you will receive your membership card in the mail, and you can start saving money when you shop.

Sincerely,

Dave Wellborn

Dave Wellborn
Owner, Natural Foods

ENCLOSURE

149. What is the purpose of the letter?

(A) To apologize to a customer
(B) To promote a discount program
(C) To announce an upcoming sale
(D) To approve a request

150. What is included with the letter?

(A) A membership card
(B) A product sample
(C) An application form
(D) A store catalog

Questions 151-152 refer to the following e-mail.

To	All Sales Staff
From	Judith Ralston
Date	September 19
Subject	Important News

Hello all,

There was a mistake in our ad in yesterday's issue of the *Eagleton Daily*. It said our fall sale will begin on September 20; not on October 14. The *Eagleton Daily* will run a correction in tomorrow's paper, but not everyone who comes to our store will have seen it. If you have any customers asking about the sale before it officially begins, please explain what happened and give them a coupon for 15 percent off of their next purchase here. Please tell any consumers with additional concerns to speak with a shift supervisor. Thank you in advance for your cooperation.

Judith Ralston
Branch Manager
Morey's Electronics

151. What is mentioned about the *Eagleton Daily*?

(A) It misprinted the starting date of a special promotion.
(B) It runs ads for Morey's Electronics in every issue.
(C) It offered a 15 percent discount to first-time customers.
(D) It apologized to Ms. Ralston for an error.

152. What does Ms. Ralston instruct the sales staff to do?

(A) Show customers how to use some items
(B) Direct customers with further questions to a manager
(C) Refer customers to advertisements on a store Web site
(D) Tell customers about a membership program

Questions 153-155 refer to the following article.

Portland Daily Culture News
Staff Writer Terrence Park

(May 10) Rose Purcell, the present executive manager at the Museum of Natural History in Dallas, has accepted a new position in Portland. —[1]—. She will become the director at the Portland Museum starting on June 1. —[2]—. Ms. Purcell is a native of Portland but has lived away from the city for the past 20 years. Portland Museum's board of directors decided to hire Ms. Purcell not only for her local connections but also for her knowledge. They had been searching for someone to ensure that the upcoming expansion of its facility will go smoothly. —[3]—. "I'm excited to be a part of an institution that has been an asset to this community since I was a child," she commented. The Portland Museum will be featuring several new exhibits in the following months. —[4]—. General admission prices will remain the same at $15 per person. Ms. Purcell stated that she is looking forward to this new opportunity and her return to her native city.

153. Why was the article written?

(A) To review Portland's newest tourist attractions
(B) To discuss an executive's career decision
(C) To explain why a museum will close
(D) To announce the relocation of a local business

154. What does the Portland Museum plan to do?

(A) Renovate a facility
(B) Increase admission prices
(C) Hire more tour guides
(D) Hold a board election

155. In which of the positions marked [1], [2], [3], and [4] does the following sentence best belong?

"Some of the displays will require an additional fee to view."

(A) [1]
(B) [2]
(C) [3]
(D) [4]

Questions 156-157 refer to the following text message chain.

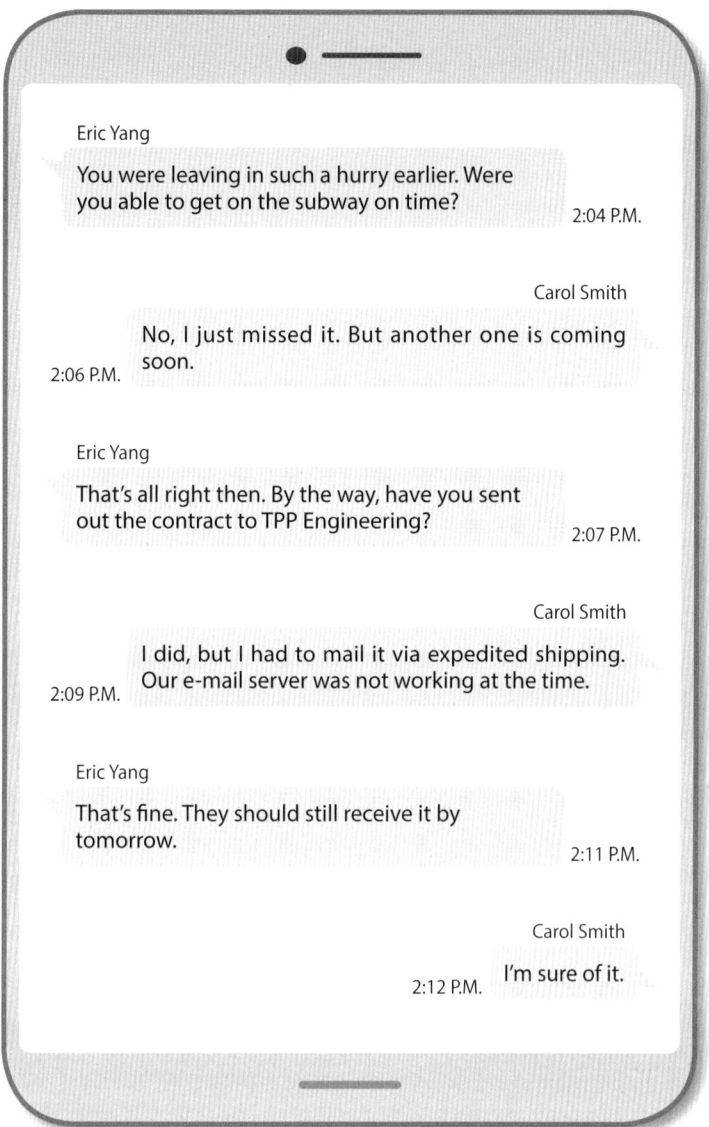

156. Where most likely is Ms. Smith?

(A) At a subway station
(B) At TPP Engineering's office
(C) At her desk
(D) At a restaurant

157. At 2:12 P.M., what does Ms. Smith imply when she writes, "I'm sure of it"?

(A) A package will be delivered on time.
(B) A promotion will be successful.
(C) Some contract terms must be changed.
(D) Expedited shipping is not that expensive.

Questions 158-161 refer to the following online chat discussion.

Rusty Barker 8:35 A.M.
Hi, everyone. It's been a while since we had our last discussion regarding this summer's festival. I've got some great news. Nancy, why don't you tell everyone?

Nancy Green 8:37 A.M.
Sure. Our request to have the festival at Canary Park was approved by the city council last night!

James Watson 8:38 A.M.
That's wonderful!

Jane Hampton 8:40 A.M.
That is good news. I was under the impression that it wasn't going to happen.

Nancy Green 8:42 A.M.
We were finally able to persuade the council when we agreed to limit the number of attendees to 3,000 each day.

Rusty Barker 8:44 A.M.
Does anyone else have some news to share?

James Watson 8:48 A.M.
Pete's Fine Dining is already set to have a booth at the festival. It's one of the most popular places in the city. I should also have answers from several other eateries within the week.

Jane Hampton 8:49 A.M.
Danielle Johnson has tentatively agreed to be one of the headliners at the concert on the last night. I'm still trying to get some other artists to perform.

Rusty Barker 8:51 A.M.
Great. I know a lot of people would like to see her sing. OK, everyone. Well done.

158. What is the online chat discussion about?
 (A) An online seminar
 (B) A product launch
 (C) An outdoor event
 (D) A new safety regulation

159. At 8:40 A.M., what does Ms. Hampton mean when she writes, "I was under the impression that it wasn't going to happen"?
 (A) She was not sure a meeting would be held.
 (B) She was not sure a vendor would participate.
 (C) She believed a price would be increased.
 (D) She believed a request would be denied.

160. What is Mr. Watson expecting?
 (A) Confirmation of attendance numbers
 (B) Responses from some establishments
 (C) Cancellations from some ticket holders
 (D) Revisions to a timetable

161. What most likely is Ms. Johnson's profession?
 (A) Singer
 (B) Maintenance worker
 (C) Journalist
 (D) City council member

Questions 162-164 refer to the following Web page.

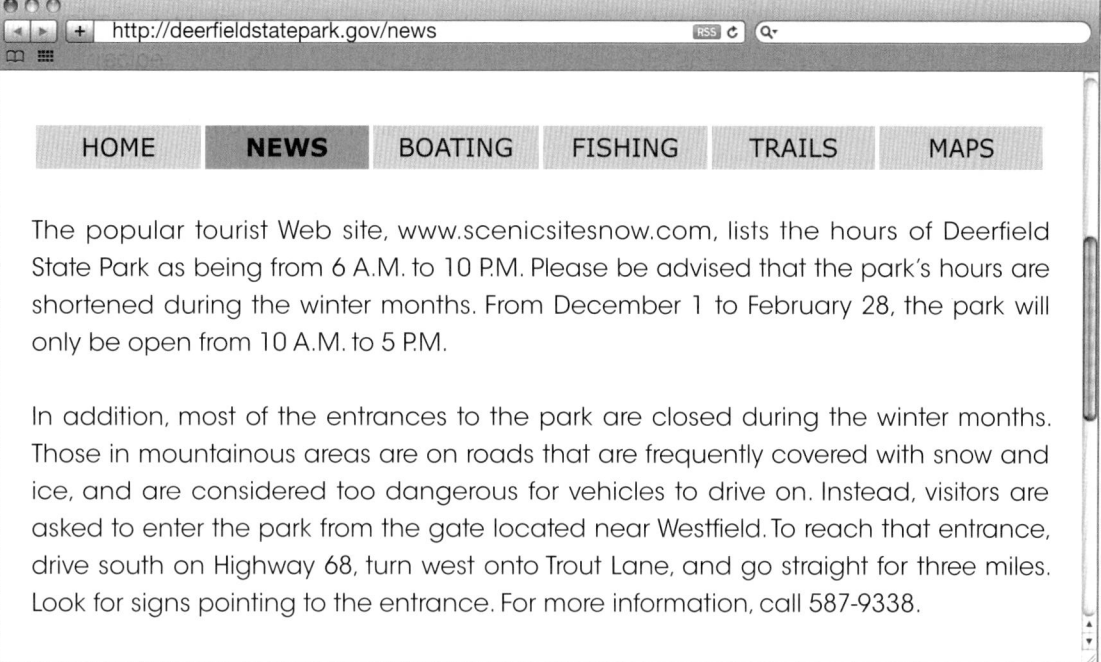

162. For whom is the notice most likely intended?

    (A) Road construction workers
    (B) Park guests
    (C) Seasonal staff
    (D) Westfield commuters

163. What is implied about the Web site, www.scenicsitesnow.com?

    (A) It was recently created.
    (B) It is managed by Deerfield State Park employees.
    (C) It lists incorrect information.
    (D) It has details on parks in other countries.

164. What is included in the notice?

    (A) Directions to the park
    (B) Descriptions of job positions
    (C) A list of monthly events
    (D) Updates on trail renovations

GO ON TO THE NEXT PAGE

Questions 165-168 refer to the following e-mail.

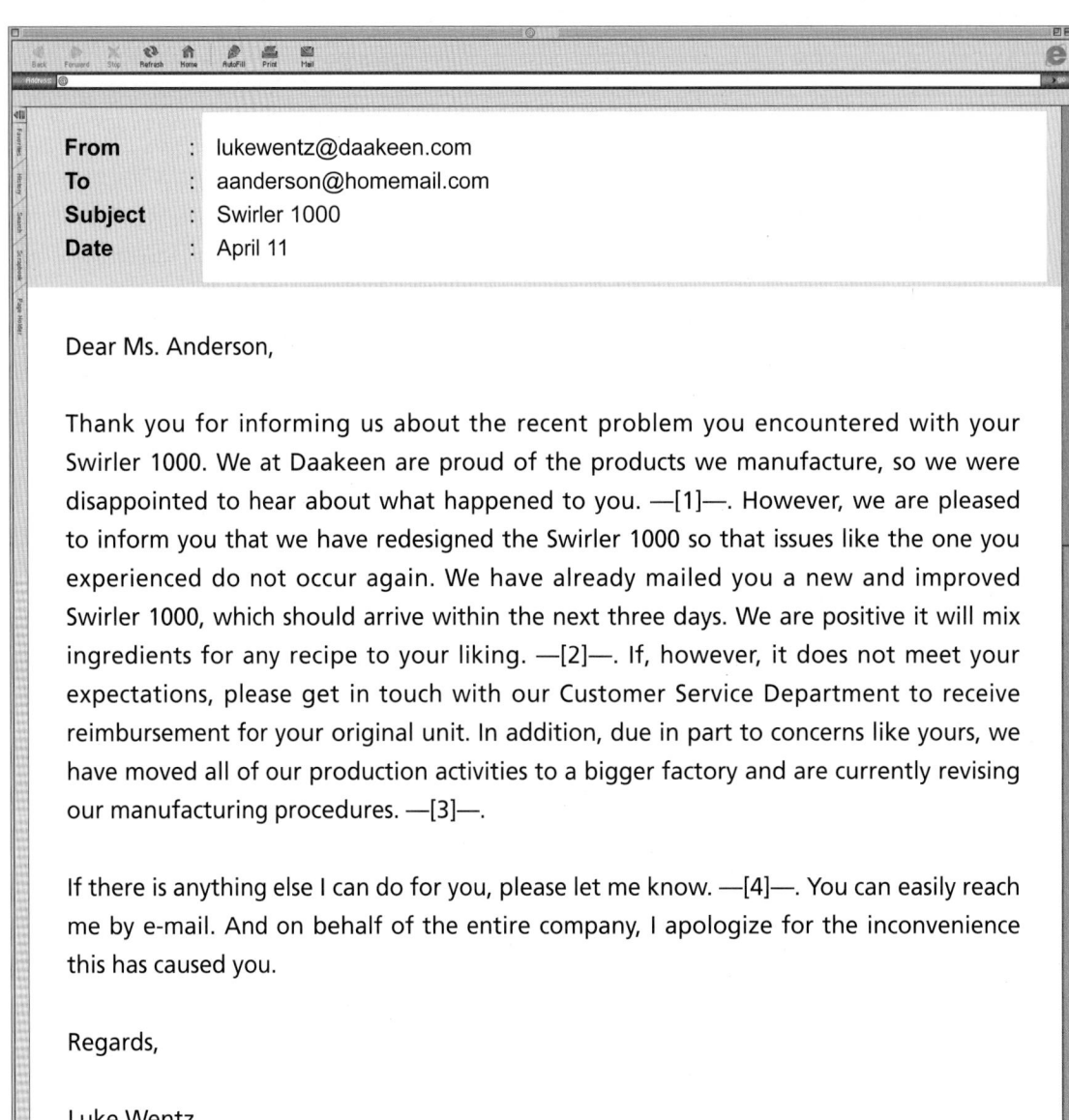

From : lukewentz@daakeen.com
To : aanderson@homemail.com
Subject : Swirler 1000
Date : April 11

Dear Ms. Anderson,

Thank you for informing us about the recent problem you encountered with your Swirler 1000. We at Daakeen are proud of the products we manufacture, so we were disappointed to hear about what happened to you. —[1]—. However, we are pleased to inform you that we have redesigned the Swirler 1000 so that issues like the one you experienced do not occur again. We have already mailed you a new and improved Swirler 1000, which should arrive within the next three days. We are positive it will mix ingredients for any recipe to your liking. —[2]—. If, however, it does not meet your expectations, please get in touch with our Customer Service Department to receive reimbursement for your original unit. In addition, due in part to concerns like yours, we have moved all of our production activities to a bigger factory and are currently revising our manufacturing procedures. —[3]—.

If there is anything else I can do for you, please let me know. —[4]—. You can easily reach me by e-mail. And on behalf of the entire company, I apologize for the inconvenience this has caused you.

Regards,

Luke Wentz
Customer Service Representative
Daakeen Products

165. Why did Mr. Wentz send the e-mail to Ms. Anderson?

(A) To describe a new item
(B) To request a product sample
(C) To respond to a complaint
(D) To explain a return policy

166. What most likely is the Swirler 1000?

(A) A food processor
(B) An air conditioner
(C) A dishwasher
(D) A refrigerator

167. What is NOT mentioned as a solution to the problem?

(A) Providing a refund
(B) Repairing a product for free
(C) Improving manufacturing processes
(D) Delivering a replacement product

168. In which of the positions marked [1], [2], [3], and [4] does the following sentence best belong?

"An operations manager will come by the facility occasionally to make sure that everything is running smoothly."

(A) [1]
(B) [2]
(C) [3]
(D) [4]

GO ON TO THE NEXT PAGE

Questions 169-172 refer to the following article.

Airport Expansion Underway

(October 11) – The $900 million expansion of Richmond Airport has begun. The project will add a new terminal to accommodate overseas flights by December of next year.

While the new terminal project has been planned for some time, airport authorities have held off on approval for an additional runway. Flights into Richmond will reach the airport's capacity within four years unless a new runway is constructed.

Due to space restrictions, a new runway may have to extend out into the Atlantic Ocean. Grover Engineering has been contracted to determine if this construction is feasible. Engineers from the company will conduct extensive research for five months and present the results to the city council.

Runways partially over water have been built elsewhere. Authorities are currently in Portugal studying the award-winning design of one such airport on the island of Madeira.

---

169. Why is Richmond Airport undergoing an expansion?

(A) To lower the number of flight delays
(B) To offer better services than nearby communities
(C) To accommodate international flights
(D) To cater to the growing number of residents in neighboring towns

170. The word "capacity" in paragraph 2, line 6, is closest in meaning to

(A) readiness
(B) limit
(C) approach
(D) ability

171. What has Grover Engineering been hired to do?

(A) To redesign the air traffic control tower
(B) To help reduce the traffic around the airport
(C) To determine whether a runway can be built
(D) To review plans to repair a facility

172. What is implied about Richmond Airport?

(A) It is situated on the coast.
(B) It was opened last December.
(C) It will generate $900 million in revenue.
(D) It has received an award.

Questions 173-175 refer to the following notice.

Milan Pharmaceutical Convention

Event Hall Rules
Exhibitor Pass Guidelines

Only vendors from approved companies, convention attendees, and personnel are permitted to enter the event hall. Everyone in the event hall must have their pass on them at all times.

- Vendor passes will be provided to the companies' main contacts to give to their booth staff.
- The number of passes that will be given will be determined by the size of the booth a company has reserved.
- People in the event hall without the proper credentials will be asked to leave.
- Improper use of vendor passes or submission of false documents will result in immediate removal from the convention area.

173. Why was the notice written?

 (A) To identify who is allowed in the event hall
 (B) To explain a change in the convention's schedule
 (C) To give instructions on how to set up a booth
 (D) To specify which facilities can be used by attendees

174. How will individual team members receive their passes?

 (A) Company representatives will distribute the passes to them.
 (B) They will get the passes when they sign in at the convention's front desk.
 (C) They can print the passes from a Web site.
 (D) Customized passes will be mailed to their office.

175. How can a company have more employees work at the convention?

 (A) By filling out a special form
 (B) By contacting the convention staff
 (C) By requesting extra passes online
 (D) By reserving a larger space at the event

GO ON TO THE NEXT PAGE

Questions 176-180 refer to the following e-mails.

To	samanthawake@pto.com
From	shawn_j@gwo.org
Date	August 20
Subject	GWO

Dear Ms. Wake,

Thank you for agreeing to assist me with the preparations for the Global Writers' Organization (GWO) Conference to be held on November 2-3. I would like to provide you with some information about what is on the agenda.

I get the sense that our preferred choice, Nelson Beale, is probably out of our price range. But I'm going to try to convince local businesses to provide some funding. If we're able to get these resources, I'll focus on securing Mr. Beale. Should we be unsuccessful, I'll contact Anna Porter. I hope you will be able to get enough panelists for the "Negotiating a Contract" session. Let's keep in touch.

Regards,

Shawn Jacobs
Organizer, GWO Conference

To	: n_beale@promail.com
From	: shawn_j@gwo.org
Date	: September 9
Subject	: GWO Conference
Attachment	: nb_agreement

Mr. Beale,

I am writing to confirm that you will be the keynote speaker at the Global Writers' Organization (GWO) Conference in November. As we agreed in our last discussion, you will speak for 40-45 minutes on the first day of the event. We will have multimedia facilities available as well, should your presentation require them. We would also like for you to participate in the panel discussion entitled "Negotiating a Contract." We believe your years of experience with publishers will be of great value in this session. The discussion will be held on November 3.

We will cover the costs of your flight, hotel accommodations, food, and other basic expenses. However, please be aware that a return flight ticket will only be offered if you attend both days of the conference. Otherwise, we will only pay for a one-way ticket. Please let me know about this as soon as you can so that I can make the necessary arrangements.

To agree to these terms, please print out and sign the attached contract. You can fax it to me at (908) 435-5858.

Sincerely,

Shawn Jacobs
Organizer, GWO Conference

176. What is the purpose of the first e-mail?

(A) To ask for funding
(B) To discuss a new agreement
(C) To share details of an event
(D) To review some job candidates

177. In the first e-mail, the word "sense" in paragraph 2, line 1, is closest in meaning to

(A) point
(B) recognition
(C) touch
(D) feeling

178. What is most likely true about Mr. Jacobs?

(A) He plans to eat lunch with Mr. Beale on November 2.
(B) He will organize a career workshop.
(C) His organization received private contributions.
(D) His suggestion for a speaker was not accepted.

179. What is suggested about Mr. Beale?

(A) He has worked with many publishing companies.
(B) He is a well-known reporter.
(C) He regularly attends conferences organized by the GWO.
(D) He will speak for 80 minutes.

180. According to the second e-mail, what must Mr. Beale do to have all of the airfare costs paid for by the GWO?

(A) Finalize a travel schedule by September 30
(B) Take part in the entire conference
(C) Provide his bank account information for reimbursement
(D) Turn in all of his receipts

GO ON TO THE NEXT PAGE

Questions 181-185 refer to the following e-mail and magazine index.

To	joesampson@mymail.com
From	paulac@delectabledesserts.com
Date	July 11
Subject	Contest results

Dear Mr. Sampson,

I'm pleased to let you know that your submission, "Sampson's Apple-Cranberry Delight", has been chosen as the winner of our Dessert Showdown. As a result, your recipe will be included in the September issue of our magazine. Please be aware that we might have to shorten the name of your recipe for editorial purposes.

We do need some information from you before we can publish the recipe. You mentioned that you could add walnuts or pecans to the recipe. Can you let me know how many walnuts or pecans should be used? In addition, what is the best way of preserving these jellies? I would appreciate this information.

One more thing: please send a recent photograph of yourself. We always place a photo of the creator next to the recipe.

Sincerely,

Paula Corker
Delectable Desserts Magazine

***Delectable Desserts Magazine* Table of Contents**

September, Issue 87

10	Pecan Squares: Experience the big taste of pecan pie, but in small bite-sized pieces.
17	Fruit Medley: Need to put something together just minutes before a party?
28	Three-Flavor Cake: Enjoy a burst of flavor with this impressive cake.
39	Key Lime Pie: Try this new recipe for an old favorite.
51	Apple-Cranberry Delight: Get a taste of fall's finest fruits in the form of small jellies.
74	Peach Cobbler: Peach season is coming to an end, so don't wait to make this dessert that will get everyone's taste buds excited.

181. What is the purpose of the e-mail?

(A) To invite Mr. Sampson to tour a facility
(B) To ask Mr. Sampson to send another recipe
(C) To confirm details of a recipe
(D) To give instructions on how to claim a prize

182. In the e-mail, the word "submission" in paragraph 1, line 1, is closest in meaning to

(A) compliance
(B) entry in a contest
(C) article for a magazine
(D) resignation

183. What does Ms. Corker NOT ask Mr. Sampson to provide?

(A) A new name for his recipe
(B) A picture of himself
(C) The proper method of storage
(D) The amounts of some ingredients

184. On what page does Mr. Sampson's recipe appear?

(A) 10
(B) 28
(C) 51
(D) 74

185. What is indicated about the recipe on page 17?

(A) It is a healthy choice.
(B) It can be made quickly.
(C) It has few ingredients.
(D) It was designed by a popular chef.

GO ON TO THE NEXT PAGE

Questions 186-190 refer to the following memo, e-mail, and article.

To: All Employees
From: Ursula Jarvis, CEO
Subject: Information
Date: April 11

On Monday, May 16, a journalist from *Technology Today* will visit our factory to see where we make our solar panels. He will be accompanied by one of our public relations officials. You are free to speak with the journalist about your daily work activities, but you should not provide any information about the specifications of our solar panels. We don't want our competitors finding about our new technology. Please read over our media policies on page 8 of the company handbook. We will send you any updates regarding the event via e-mail.

We appreciate your cooperation in this matter.

To	David Waterford <davidw@solarenergon.com>
From	Lance McCullers <lance_mccullers@technologytoday.com>
Date	April 12
Subject	Visit

Dear Mr. Waterford,

Due to an urgent project deadline, I have no choice but to postpone my visit to your plant. I can, however, come by on the following dates: Tuesday, May 17, in the morning, Wednesday, May 18, in the afternoon, or Thursday, May 19, in the morning.

I will also be bringing Mindy Hamilton, our company photographer, with me. She has been informed that she may not take any pictures of the assembly process and will only photograph the exteriors of your buildings as well as the employees themselves.

Regards,

Lance McCullers
Technology Today

A Breakthrough in Solar Panel Technology?

By Lance McCullers

June 3

As a company that is part of the renewable energy sector, Solar Energon practices the same principles it is dedicated to enabling. The hot sun reflects off panels on the roof of this small company located in a suburb of Sydney, Australia. That sunlight powers everything that's going on inside this remarkable plant.

"We at Solar Energon are proud to have the best solar panels around," said Ivan Tunsil, as he guided me through the factory one afternoon. "Thanks to a discovery we made, our panels are more than twice as efficient as other products available today. At the same time, we are able to sell our panels for 80 percent of what the average one costs."

It may sound strange that the company has both improved the product and lowered the price, but that's what has happened. They are also experimenting with different uses for solar energy, such as designing solar bars for windows. "Future possibilities are almost limitless," CEO Ursula Jarvis said. Keep an eye out on this up-and-coming company. It appears that the future is bright at Solar Energon.

---

186. Why was the memo sent?

(A) To publicize a new factory location
(B) To discuss some research findings
(C) To give instructions for talking to a reporter
(D) To describe the functions of a new machine

187. When did Mr. McCullers most likely visit the factory?

(A) On May 16
(B) On May 17
(C) On May 18
(D) On May 19

188. What does the article indicate about Solar Energon?

(A) It is testing new types of products.
(B) It will purchase new equipment.
(C) It is undergoing renovations.
(D) It will revise its safety procedures.

189. What is implied about Mr. Tunsil?

(A) He was recently hired by Solar Energon.
(B) He took a photo with Mr. Waterford.
(C) He is a native of Sydney.
(D) He is involved in public relations.

190. In the article, the word "bright" in paragraph 3, line 11, is closest in meaning to

(A) shiny
(B) promising
(C) brilliant
(D) cheerful

Questions 191-195 refer to the following letter, e-mail, and advertisement.

Dear Supporter of the Jackson Fine Arts Center,

As you may know, our annual Jackson Fine Arts Center (JFAC) fundraiser dinner is coming up. This year, we are raising money for our center's newest jazz program. We would like to invite you to help sponsor this year's event. The entire community, as well as local news stations, will be in attendance. Being a sponsor will give your business great visibility.

Here is a list of the sponsorship options:

Signature Sponsor: $7,500
-Company's name and logo will appear in the headlines of all promotional materials.
-A company representative will have an opportunity to speak at the event.

Star Sponsor: $4,500
-Company name will be displayed on our Web site.
-A sponsor recognition plaque will be given.

Gold Sponsor: $2,000
-Company name will be displayed on all event posters for a year.
-Company will receive six tickets to every event at the center for a year.

Partner Sponsor: $750
-Company name will be displayed on all event posters for a year.

All contributions are accepted, and everything is going towards a great cause. Feel free to contact me should you have questions.

Regards,

Hunter Brown
JFAC Events Coordinator

To	:	hbrown@jfac.org
From	:	tswilton@molterbank.com
Date	:	10 July
Subject	:	Fundraiser details
Attachment	:	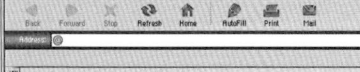 molterbank_picture

Dear Mr. Brown,

I have attached an electronic version of our firm's logo to be used in the advertising materials for your events.

In addition, James Rollins, Head of Public Relations, and his team will be attending the fundraiser. He requests that we receive pictures of his presentation via e-mail. He also asked about meeting with the director of the fine arts center. He has some suggestions on other ways we can help the center. Please let me know if this will be possible and when you would like to meet. Thank you.

Best,

Tanya Swilton, Molter Bank

Jackson Fine Arts Center Fundraising Dinner on July 22 at 5 P.M.

Sponsored by Molter Bank

If you'd like to participate in the event, please sign up by July 12 through our Web site. During the dinner, live entertainment will be provided by members of our center's newest program. Event T-shirts and other items will be on sale at the reception area.

---

191. For whom is the letter most likely intended?

(A) Local artists
(B) Financial consultants
(C) Marketing specialists
(D) Business owners

192. In the letter, the word "visibility" in paragraph 1, line 4, is closest in meaning to

(A) placement
(B) clarity
(C) attention
(D) location

193. What kind of sponsorship did Molter Bank most likely choose?

(A) Signature Sponsor
(B) Star Sponsor
(C) Gold Sponsor
(D) Partner Sponsor

194. What is suggested about James Rollins?

(A) He will be speaking at a dinner.
(B) He will be performing in a show.
(C) He organized a fundraiser.
(D) He is employed by the JFAC.

195. What is indicated about the event?

(A) It will feature a musical show.
(B) A famous photographer will be taking pictures.
(C) It will be shown on the Internet.
(D) Ms. Swilton will be giving a keynote speech.

Questions 196-200 refer to the following e-mail, Web page, and article.

To	Harriet Ramirez, CEO
From	Adrian Morales
Subject	Request
Date	October 11

Dear Ms. Ramirez,

Are you aware of the Belém Business Tournament being held next February? The tournament is organized by the Belém Chamber of Commerce and held in conjunction with the Belém Conference, one of the largest business events in the Western Hemisphere. The tournament lets entrants manage imaginary companies as they attempt to improve the financial situation and stability of their firms.

I believe that participating in this contest could be beneficial for us. First, it will provide the six employees on the team with excellent leadership training, as they will learn how to manage a company. They'll be able to use that knowledge when they return to work after the event ends. They will also learn about teamwork and improve their organizational skills, which will benefit the company as a whole. In addition, by taking part in the contest, our company would become more of a publically recognized company. Last year, 54 companies participated in the tournament, and a few months later, more than half of them reported that they had gotten more business due to the tournament's widespread media coverage.

Go to www.belemconference.org/businesstournament for more information.

Sincerely,

Adrian Morales
R&D Department, Falstaff, Inc.

---

www.belemconference.org/businesstournament

Belém Business Tournament

Registration Process

The Belém Business Tournament will be held from February 21-25. Registration for the tournament opens on December 1 and closes on February 10. Companies are limited to two teams consisting of no more than six individuals. The winner of the tournament and the two runners up will be recognized on March 3 during a ceremony at the Regentz Hotel.

Falstaff Wins Tournament

The Belém Business Tournament has been around for 15 years, but this year's event may have been the most exciting ever. Seventy-four companies entered a total of 102 teams, and the competition was fierce. A team from Guatemala that had never participated in the tournament before took first place. Adrian Morales led his team to victory in what tournament organizers say was one of the most impressive acts of leadership they have ever seen. Mr. Morales and the rest of his team will be honored with the Belém Virtual Company Award.

196. What is the goal of the participants in the Belém Business Tournament?

    (A) To operate a nonexistent company
    (B) To promote international trade
    (C) To introduce new products
    (D) To predict business trends

197. What does Mr. Morales NOT mention as a benefit of participating in the Belém Business Tournament?

    (A) Improved cooperation among staff
    (B) More public recognition of a company's services
    (C) A chance to gain leadership skills
    (D) An opportunity to invest overseas

198. What is probably true about Mr. Morales?

    (A) He no longer works at Falstaff, Inc.
    (B) He will attend a celebratory event.
    (C) He is an employee at the Regentz Hotel.
    (D) He works in the same department as Mr. Ramirez.

199. What is indicated about Falstaff, Inc.?

    (A) It is based in Guatemala.
    (B) It manufactures automobile parts.
    (C) It entered two teams in the tournament.
    (D) It is relocating to a larger building.

200. What is indicated about the most recent Belém Business Tournament?

    (A) It was broadcast in several countries around the world.
    (B) It had more participants than the previous year's competition.
    (C) It attracted more media outlets than last year's event.
    (D) It was sponsored by the Regentz Hotel.

Stop! This is the end of the test. If you finish before time is called, you may go back to Part 5, 6, and 7 and check your work.

NO TEST MATERIAL ON THIS PAGE

NO TEST MATERIAL ON THIS PAGE

Answer Keys

MP3, 해석, 해설 온라인 무료 제공
모바일: QR코드 스캔을 통해 MP3 음원 바로 듣기 / 정답, 해석, 해설 바로 보기
PC: 파고다북스 사이트(www.pagodabook.com) 접속 / 로그인 후 다운로드

Listening Comprehension

1 (A)	2 (D)	3 (D)	4 (C)	5 (D)
6 (C)	7 (A)	8 (B)	9 (B)	10 (C)
11 (C)	12 (B)	13 (C)	14 (C)	15 (A)
16 (B)	17 (A)	18 (B)	19 (A)	20 (B)
21 (A)	22 (C)	23 (C)	24 (A)	25 (C)
26 (B)	27 (A)	28 (A)	29 (C)	30 (A)
31 (C)	32 (D)	33 (A)	34 (A)	35 (D)
36 (C)	37 (D)	38 (C)	39 (A)	40 (B)
41 (D)	42 (B)	43 (B)	44 (B)	45 (A)
46 (A)	47 (B)	48 (C)	49 (D)	50 (C)
51 (D)	52 (D)	53 (D)	54 (D)	55 (B)
56 (C)	57 (D)	58 (D)	59 (A)	60 (D)
61 (C)	62 (D)	63 (B)	64 (A)	65 (D)
66 (C)	67 (D)	68 (B)	69 (A)	70 (C)
71 (C)	72 (D)	73 (A)	74 (C)	75 (D)
76 (A)	77 (C)	78 (B)	79 (D)	80 (A)
81 (D)	82 (B)	83 (A)	84 (D)	85 (D)
86 (B)	87 (C)	88 (A)	89 (B)	90 (C)
91 (A)	92 (B)	93 (C)	94 (B)	95 (D)
96 (B)	97 (D)	98 (A)	99 (D)	100 (C)

Reading Comprehension

101 (A)	102 (C)	103 (C)	104 (B)	105 (A)
106 (D)	107 (A)	108 (A)	109 (C)	110 (D)
111 (C)	112 (C)	113 (C)	114 (C)	115 (B)
116 (D)	117 (A)	118 (C)	119 (B)	120 (C)
121 (B)	122 (C)	123 (C)	124 (C)	125 (B)
126 (D)	127 (C)	128 (C)	129 (A)	130 (B)
131 (B)	132 (C)	133 (A)	134 (D)	135 (A)
136 (D)	137 (D)	138 (C)	139 (D)	140 (A)
141 (C)	142 (C)	143 (D)	144 (A)	145 (C)
146 (B)	147 (C)	148 (A)	149 (B)	150 (C)
151 (A)	152 (B)	153 (B)	154 (A)	155 (D)
156 (A)	157 (A)	158 (C)	159 (D)	160 (B)
161 (A)	162 (B)	163 (C)	164 (A)	165 (C)
166 (A)	167 (B)	168 (C)	169 (C)	170 (B)
171 (C)	172 (A)	173 (A)	174 (A)	175 (D)
176 (C)	177 (D)	178 (C)	179 (A)	180 (B)
181 (C)	182 (B)	183 (A)	184 (C)	185 (B)
186 (C)	187 (C)	188 (A)	189 (D)	190 (B)
191 (D)	192 (C)	193 (A)	194 (A)	195 (A)
196 (A)	197 (D)	198 (B)	199 (A)	200 (B)

파고다토익
시험 직전
마무리 TEST 1
모의고사

초판 1쇄 인쇄   2017년 12월 27일
초판 1쇄 발행   2018년 1월 2일
초판 16쇄 발행   2024년 9월 30일

지 은 이	파고다교육그룹 언어교육연구소
펴 낸 이	박경실
펴 낸 곳	**PAGODA Books** 파고다북스
출판등록	2005년 5월 27일 제 300-2005-90호
주 소	06614 서울특별시 서초구 강남대로 419, 19층(서초동, 파고다타워)
전 화	(02) 6940-4070
팩 스	(02) 536-0660
홈페이지	www.pagodabook.com
저작권자	ⓒ 2018 파고다아카데미

이 책의 저작권은 저자와 출판사에 있습니다. 서면에 의한 저작권자와 출판사의 허락 없이
내용의 일부 혹은 전부를 인용 및 복제하거나 발췌하는 것을 금합니다.

Copyright ⓒ 2018 by PAGODA Academy

All rights reserved. No part of this publication may be reproduced, stored
in a retrieval system, or transmitted, in any form, or by any means, electronic,
mechanical, photocopying, recording or otherwise, without the prior written
permission of the copyright holder and the publisher.

ISBN 978-89-6281-808-6 (13740)

파고다북스	www.pagodabook.com
파고다 어학원	www.pagoda21.com
파고다 인강	www.pagodastar.com
테스트 클리닉	www.testclinic.com

| 낙장 및 파본은 구매처에서 교환해 드립니다.

PAGODA Books

파고다토익
시험 직전
마무리 TEST 2
모의고사

해설 바로 보기   음원 바로 듣기

PAGODA Books

시험 진행 안내

❶ 시험 시간: 120분(2시간)
- Listening Comprehension 100문제: 45분
- Reading Comprehension 100문제: 75분
- L/C 진행 후 휴식 시간 없이 바로 R/C 진행

❷ 준비물
- 컴퓨터용 사인펜 또는 연필

❸ 시험 응시 준수 사항
- 시험 시작 10분 전 입실 (이후에는 입실 불가)
- 종료 30분 전과 10분 전에 시험 종료 공지함
- 휴대전화의 전원을 꺼둘 것

❹ OMR 답안지 표기 요령
- 반드시 컴퓨터용 사인펜 또는 연필로 표기
- 개인정보, 문제번호, 단체명, 문제번호, 학과(부서) 및 학번코드 표기
  (학과(부서)코드는 별도 공지)

※ 개인정보, 문제번호, 학과(부서)코드, 주민등록번호를 틀리게 표기했을 경우 채점 및 성적 확인이 불가능하므로 주의하시기 바랍니다.

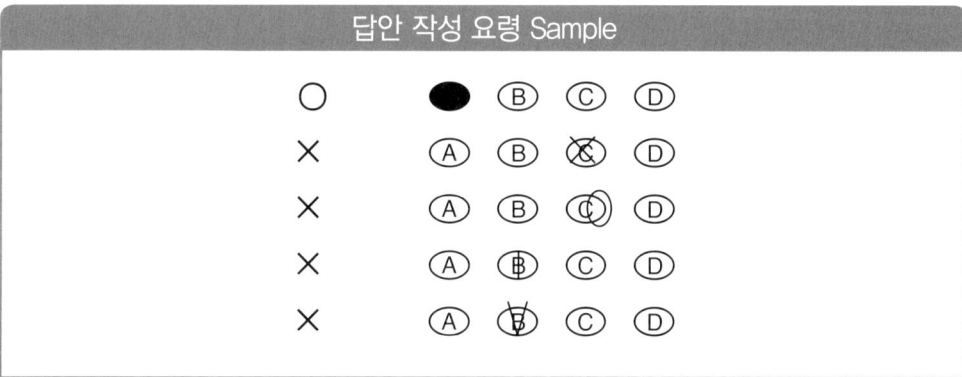

LISTENING TEST

In the Listening test, you will be asked to demonstrate how well you understand spoken English. The entire listening test will last approximately 45 minutes. There are four parts, and directions are given for each part. You must mark your answers on the separate answer sheet. Do not write your answers in your test book.

PART 1

Directions: For each question in this part, you will hear four statements about a picture in your test book. When you hear the statements, you must select the one statement that best describes what you see in the picture. Then find the number of the question on your answer sheet and mark your answer. The statements will not be printed in your test book and will be spoken only one time.

Statement (B), "A man is pointing at a document," is the best description of the picture, so you should select answer (B) and mark it on your answer sheet.

1.

2.

GO ON TO THE NEXT PAGE

3.

4.

5.

6.

PART 2

Directions: You will hear a question or statement and three responses spoken in English. They will not be printed in your test book and will be spoken only one time. Select the best response to the question or statement and mark the letter (A), (B), or (C) on your answer sheet.

7. Mark your answer on your answer sheet.
8. Mark your answer on your answer sheet.
9. Mark your answer on your answer sheet.
10. Mark your answer on your answer sheet.
11. Mark your answer on your answer sheet.
12. Mark your answer on your answer sheet.
13. Mark your answer on your answer sheet.
14. Mark your answer on your answer sheet.
15. Mark your answer on your answer sheet.
16. Mark your answer on your answer sheet.
17. Mark your answer on your answer sheet.
18. Mark your answer on your answer sheet.
19. Mark your answer on your answer sheet.
20. Mark your answer on your answer sheet.
21. Mark your answer on your answer sheet.
22. Mark your answer on your answer sheet.
23. Mark your answer on your answer sheet.
24. Mark your answer on your answer sheet.
25. Mark your answer on your answer sheet.
26. Mark your answer on your answer sheet.
27. Mark your answer on your answer sheet.
28. Mark your answer on your answer sheet.
29. Mark your answer on your answer sheet.
30. Mark your answer on your answer sheet.
31. Mark your answer on your answer sheet.

PART 3

Directions: You will hear some conversations between two or more people. You will be asked to answer three questions about what the speakers say in each conversation. Select the best response to each question and mark the letter (A), (B), (C), or (D) on your answer sheet. The conversations will not be printed in your test book and will be spoken only one time.

32. Who most likely is the woman?
    (A) A real estate agent
    (B) A tour operator
    (C) A customer service associate
    (D) A maintenance worker

33. What does the man want to do?
    (A) Change the location of a delivery
    (B) Purchase a different product
    (C) Send an updated invoice
    (D) Invite coworkers to an event

34. What does the woman offer to do?
    (A) Provide a refund
    (B) Reserve an item
    (C) Contact a courier service
    (D) Give a special discount

35. What will the woman do next week?
    (A) Go on a trip
    (B) Renovate an office
    (C) Hold a training session
    (D) Work in a new position

36. Why has the woman been busy?
    (A) She is organizing a seminar.
    (B) She is preparing to move.
    (C) She is interviewing job candidates.
    (D) She is finishing a report.

37. What does the man offer to do for the woman?
    (A) Install some equipment
    (B) Call a company
    (C) Bring some supplies
    (D) Send a document

38. What do the women invite the man to do?
    (A) Participate in a survey
    (B) Have a meal with colleagues
    (C) Organize a company picnic
    (D) Give a talk to some workers

39. What problem does the man mention?
    (A) Some equipment is broken.
    (B) Some documents are missing.
    (C) There is not enough time.
    (D) There are too many people.

40. What does the man say he will do?
    (A) Change a reservation
    (B) Inspect a machine
    (C) Send out an e-mail
    (D) Talk to a supervisor

41. What is the main topic of the conversation?
    (A) A building floor plan
    (B) A conference center opening
    (C) A safety inspection
    (D) A construction permit

42. What is the woman concerned about?
    (A) The amount of expenses
    (B) The date of a project
    (C) The location of a room
    (D) The number of guests

43. What will the woman do next?
    (A) Submit a proposal
    (B) Confirm a change
    (C) Book a venue
    (D) Arrange a meeting

GO ON TO THE NEXT PAGE

44. Why is the woman calling?

(A) To reschedule a meeting
(B) To compliment an employee
(C) To discuss a contract
(D) To offer an apology

45. What do the speakers imply about Tanya Hart?

(A) She has international clients.
(B) She will receive a bonus.
(C) She has good ideas.
(D) She will retire soon.

46. What does the man say he will do in the afternoon?

(A) Update a manual
(B) Prepare a presentation
(C) Give a colleague a message
(D) Send an office some supplies

47. What event are the speakers discussing?

(A) A retirement party
(B) An awards ceremony
(C) A birthday celebration
(D) A company anniversary

48. Why does the man say, "you know about the vice president, right"?

(A) To advise a worker to arrive early
(B) To indicate that a mistake has been made
(C) To request more funding for an event
(D) To suggest that a different venue be found

49. What will the man most likely do next?

(A) Revise a schedule
(B) Call a business
(C) Attend a meeting
(D) Send a payment

50. Why does the man say he was disappointed with the hotel?

(A) Its services were too expensive.
(B) Its location was far from downtown.
(C) Some employees were not helpful.
(D) Some facilities were not clean.

51. What does the woman say will be done?

(A) A voucher will be given.
(B) A taxi will be reserved.
(C) Some workers will be trained.
(D) Some information will be checked.

52. What does the man ask for?

(A) A bigger room
(B) Wireless Internet
(C) A Web site address
(D) Reimbursement

53. Why will the man go to Rome?

(A) To conduct research
(B) To visit relatives
(C) To participate in a conference
(D) To interview for a job

54. What does the woman explain?

(A) How to install a mobile application
(B) How to use a shuttle service
(C) How to obtain a ticket
(D) How to receive a discount

55. What does the woman suggest to the man?

(A) Postponing a trip
(B) Looking for other suppliers
(C) Taking a taxi together
(D) Claiming some expenses

56. What are the speakers discussing?

(A) A phone service plan
(B) A budget proposal
(C) A corporate policy
(D) A staff workshop

57. Why does the woman say, "What if I have to make a doctor's appointment"?

(A) To ask about an online tool
(B) To reschedule a meeting
(C) To suggest a new idea
(D) To express a concern

58. What does the man say about some employees?

(A) They require more training.
(B) They waste time at work.
(C) They are late for meetings.
(D) They do not exercise regularly.

---

59. What has the woman done?

(A) Edited a commercial
(B) Delivered a television
(C) Reviewed a contract
(D) Conducted a survey

60. What does the man imply when he says, "Tricia has years of experience in TV advertising"?

(A) Tricia should give a presentation.
(B) Tricia would offer useful feedback.
(C) Tricia is searching for a new job.
(D) Tricia will be promoted.

61. What does the woman say will take place on Friday?

(A) A client meeting
(B) A job interview
(C) A product launch
(D) A building tour

62. What does the man want to purchase?

(A) Restaurant uniforms
(B) Gardening equipment
(C) Outdoor furniture
(D) Food supplies

63. Why will the man probably receive a discount?

(A) He is a regular customer.
(B) He is placing a large order.
(C) A delivery arrived late.
(D) An item was damaged.

64. According to the man, what will happen later this month?

(A) A promotional event will start.
(B) Renovation work will begin.
(C) A business will be opened.
(D) New employees will be hired.

GO ON TO THE NEXT PAGE

ER101	Blocked pump
ER102	Fan not working
ER103	Pressure sensor malfunction
ER104	Faulty water heater

65. What most likely is the man's job?

(A) Store employee
(B) Factory inspector
(C) Corporate trainer
(D) Professional photographer

66. Look at the graphic. Which error code is the dishwasher showing?

(A) ER101
(B) ER102
(C) ER103
(D) ER104

67. What will the man probably do next?

(A) Demonstrate a device
(B) Issue a full refund
(C) Schedule an appointment
(D) Exchange an item

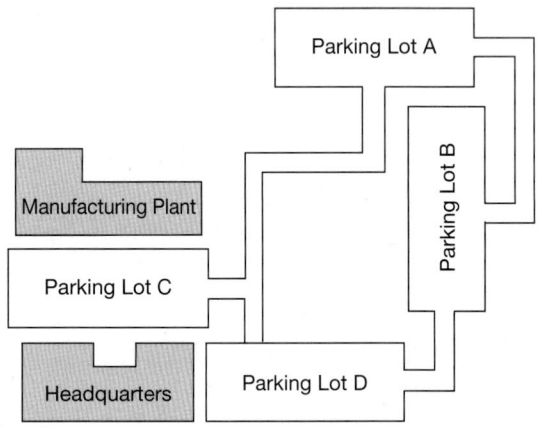

68. Look at the graphic. Which parking lot will NOT be available?

(A) A
(B) B
(C) C
(D) D

69. What concern does the man mention?

(A) Cold building temperatures
(B) High parking charges
(C) Loud construction noises
(D) Unsafe road conditions

70. According to the woman, what will the company do?

(A) Offer employee discounts
(B) Extend a project deadline
(C) Provide a shuttle bus
(D) Install new windows

PART 4

Directions: You will hear some talks given by a single speaker. You will be asked to answer three questions about what the speaker says in each talk. Select the best response to each question and mark the letter (A), (B), (C), or (D) on your answer sheet. The talks will not be printed in your test book and will be spoken only one time.

71. Where does the man most likely work?

    (A) At a moving company
    (B) At an accounting firm
    (C) At a furniture store
    (D) At a post office

72. What problem is mentioned?

    (A) An item has been damaged.
    (B) Some merchandise is unavailable.
    (C) An invoice has not been paid.
    (D) Some documents are missing.

73. Why does the man ask the woman to return his call?

    (A) To discuss a special offer
    (B) To select a product size
    (C) To check her delivery date
    (D) To receive her e-mail address

74. Where most likely is the talk being given?

    (A) At a conference center
    (B) At a Web design agency
    (C) At a medical clinic
    (D) At a construction firm

75. What does the speaker say will happen on July 9?

    (A) Construction work will begin.
    (B) Some software will be ready to use.
    (C) A new store will open for business.
    (D) A Web site will be launched.

76. What will the listeners probably do next?

    (A) Drop off some cards
    (B) Set up some equipment
    (C) Revise a report
    (D) Participate in a discussion

77. What type of event is the speaker discussing?

    (A) A corporate picnic
    (B) A grand opening
    (C) A professional gathering
    (D) An awards ceremony

78. What does the speaker instruct the listeners to do?

    (A) Update a list
    (B) Clean up an area
    (C) Register early
    (D) Check IDs

79. What can listeners do at 10 A.M.?

    (A) Take photographs
    (B) Join a tour
    (C) Attend a reception
    (D) Watch presentations

80. What is the message about?

    (A) A welcome meal
    (B) A training seminar
    (C) A charity fundraiser
    (D) A retirement party

81. What does the speaker imply when he says, "there will be 30 people attending"?

    (A) The budget may be exceeded.
    (B) A venue is not large enough.
    (C) Some people have not been invited.
    (D) An event should be canceled.

82. What is the listener asked to do?

    (A) Reserve some tickets
    (B) Inspect a facility
    (C) Contact some businesses
    (D) Pick up a guest

GO ON TO THE NEXT PAGE

83. What is the main topic of the talk?

(A) New computer products
(B) Monthly sales figures
(C) An upcoming merger
(D) A technology conference

84. What does the speaker ask the listeners to do?

(A) Revise a report
(B) Visit some stores
(C) Speak with a manager
(D) Learn about some items

85. According to the speaker, what will take place later in the week?

(A) A product launch
(B) A training session
(C) A department meeting
(D) A safety inspection

86. What does the speaker inform the listener about?

(A) Contacting some staff members
(B) Moving to a different workspace
(C) Reserving a meeting room
(D) Ordering office furniture

87. Why does the speaker say, "you're right by the copy machine"?

(A) To recommend making more handouts
(B) To suggest that an area is unsuitable
(C) To inquire about fixing some equipment
(D) To refuse a coworker's request

88. What will most likely happen tomorrow?

(A) A building will be renovated.
(B) A new employee will start work.
(C) A telephone line will be installed.
(D) A manufacturing plant will open.

89. Where is the introduction taking place?

(A) At a museum
(B) At a clothing store
(C) At a hotel
(D) At a fitness center

90. Who is Mr. Jones?

(A) A training instructor
(B) A branch manager
(C) A Web designer
(D) An event organizer

91. What does the speaker tell the listeners to do?

(A) Reserve their rooms
(B) Call some customers
(C) Put away their phones
(D) Display some items

Friday Schedule		
9:00 A.M.	Senior managers' meeting	Conference room
10:00 A.M.	R&D Department meeting	Room 340
10:00 A.M.	HR Department meeting	Seminar room
10:30 A.M.	Budget meeting	Room 130

92. What does the speaker say happened this morning?

(A) Some computers were updated.
(B) A new shipment arrived.
(C) Some workers were trained.
(D) A building lost electricity.

93. Look at the graphic. Where will the speaker probably go to next?

(A) Conference room
(B) Room 340
(C) Seminar room
(D) Room 130

94. According to the speaker, what will Walter Wang do today?

(A) Meet a client
(B) Place an order
(C) Answer phone calls
(D) Check some equipment

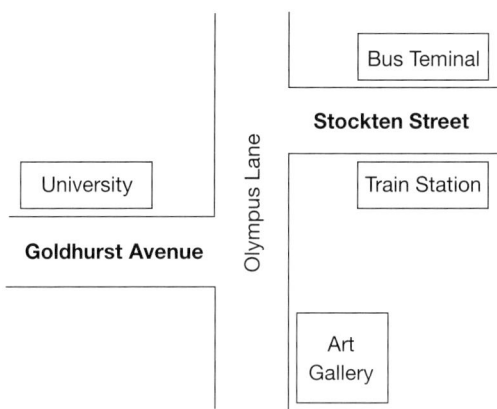

Overing Airlines

To: Seattle
Flight: O8962   Seat: 25H
Gate: B23
Boarding time: 18:30

95. Who spoke at a press conference?

(A) A city official
(B) A college professor
(C) A construction supervisor
(D) A corporate executive

96. Look at the graphic. Which building will most likely be affected first by the road closure?

(A) The bus terminal
(B) The train station
(C) The art gallery
(D) The university

97. According to the speaker, what information can listeners find on the Web site?

(A) Train schedules
(B) Job descriptions
(C) Detour sign locations
(D) Safety procedures

98. Why might some listeners visit the guest service counter?

(A) To inquire about a special meal
(B) To volunteer to go on a later flight
(C) To apply for a membership card
(D) To make shuttle service arrangements

99. Look at the graphic. According to the speaker, which information has changed?

(A) Seattle
(B) O8962
(C) B23
(D) 25H

100. What does the speaker say is the reason for the change?

(A) A malfunctioning door
(B) A sick passenger
(C) Lost luggage
(D) Inclement weather

This is the end of the Listening test. Turn to Part 5 in your test book.

GO ON TO THE NEXT PAGE

READING TEST

In the Reading test, you will read a variety of texts and answer several different types of reading comprehension questions. The entire Reading test will last 75 minutes. There are three parts, and directions are given for each part. You are encouraged to answer as many questions as possible within the time allowed.

You must mark your answers on the separate answer sheet. Do not write your answers in your test book.

PART 5

Directions: A word or phrase is missing in each of the sentences below. Four answer choices are given below each sentence. Select the best answer to complete the sentence. Then mark the letter (A), (B), (C), or (D) on your answer sheet.

101. The Quality Assurance Department should ------- be consulted when there is an increase in production errors.

    (A) eventually
    (B) once
    (C) always
    (D) precisely

102. The Kubeo Pro X987 laptop is the most powerful ------- in the store at the moment.

    (A) what
    (B) one
    (C) each
    (D) all

103. RCHM Engineering & Construction has failed to ------- positive relationships with its contractors.

    (A) maintain
    (B) maintaining
    (C) maintained
    (D) maintenance

104. The cost estimate for the landscaping project ------- any charges for additional supplies and labor.

    (A) excludes
    (B) exclusive
    (C) excluding
    (D) to exclude

105. Being a professional sports photographer, Haley Noguchi has to keep up with the latest ------- in camera technology.

    (A) developments
    (B) situations
    (C) elements
    (D) versions

106. Five employment agencies recommended candidates for the ------- recruitment needs of the Florentine Terrace Hotel.

    (A) seasonal
    (B) seasoned
    (C) seasoning
    (D) seasons

107. OWS Laboratory is researching methods to process seawater for drinking more ------- than is currently possible.

    (A) heavily
    (B) closely
    (C) slightly
    (D) efficiently

108. The new filing system adopted by Vesic Accounting Firm has turned out to be ------- effective.

    (A) further
    (B) highly
    (C) rightly
    (D) some

109. Cleary Industries awards bonuses to staff who consistently ------- the firm's expectations.
(A) conform
(B) outline
(C) exceed
(D) think

110. Renovation is ------- 75 percent done on the Mapor Inn remodeling project.
(A) now
(B) close
(C) very
(D) well

111. The questionnaire results indicate that members would ------- use the gym during weekdays than on weekends.
(A) besides
(B) cautiously
(C) beyond
(D) rather

112. Visitors can access the Regent Museum's outdoor parking lot from Lucas Street or ------- the rear entrance on Cawthra Road.
(A) through
(B) upon
(C) while
(D) as

113. The board of directors is considering several options for the headquarters' relocation, ------- is planned to take place next spring.
(A) where
(B) which
(C) when
(D) what

114. Mr. Torrance has limited training in the hotel industry, but his background in customer service is -------.
(A) extended
(B) minimal
(C) substantial
(D) enthusiastic

115. The clothing in Manuel Diego's new fall fashion collection is ------- the most creative designs of his career.
(A) within
(B) among
(C) between
(D) under

116. The study reveals that ------- in Windorville has grown steadily over the last 12 months.
(A) employs
(B) employed
(C) employers
(D) employment

117. New members will have ------- to the entire archive once their membership payment has been processed.
(A) interaction
(B) access
(C) chance
(D) permission

118. ------- Megalink's new smartphone is less expensive than other models, it is nevertheless loaded with many high-tech functions.
(A) Yet
(B) Whereas
(C) Wherever
(D) Unless

119. Due to its ------- to Santa Aves' famous beaches, the Altavilla Resort is booked year-round.
(A) base
(B) placement
(C) vacancy
(D) proximity

120. Tekmart, supplier of affordable household appliances, values ------- suggestions for increasing customer satisfaction.
(A) practice
(B) practical
(C) practices
(D) practicality

GO ON TO THE NEXT PAGE

121. The catering company has asked that we ------- any special food preferences by next Friday.

(A) exemplify
(B) specify
(C) diversify
(D) disqualify

122. Daniel Kwon, a renowned expert in alternative medicine, was the ------- presenter at the biannual Grinada Medical Workshop.

(A) extreme
(B) imminent
(C) consecutive
(D) principal

123. All of the candidates are so well-qualified that ------- the manager hires will be a good fit with the team.

(A) anyone
(B) other
(C) several
(D) someone

124. This tracking service provides ------- progress updates, so customers can monitor the status of their packages.

(A) continual
(B) mutual
(C) residual
(D) identical

125. The dinner was organized to congratulate the recently ------- senior officers on their advancement.

(A) promoting
(B) promoted
(C) promote
(D) promotes

126. All of the speakers will have finished their talks at the seminar ------- we arrive at the conference center.

(A) as soon as
(B) in a similar way
(C) by the time
(D) only when

127. To protect the roof against leaks, install stone shingles in rows that overlap by ------- 4 inches.

(A) beside
(B) instead
(C) everywhere
(D) at least

128. To reserve a conference room ------- the regular business hours, please contact us at 555-5263.

(A) outside
(B) off
(C) although
(D) alongside

129. Pulban Automotive's record sales are due to its recent ------- to prioritize business strategies.

(A) initiating
(B) initiation
(C) initiator
(D) initiative

130. The Napthum Corporation is committed to ------- that its production facilities are compliant with current environmental regulations.

(A) projecting
(B) ensuring
(C) assuming
(D) evaluating

PART 6

Directions: Read the texts that follow. A word, phrase, or sentence is missing in parts of each text. Four answer choices for each question are given below the text. Select the best answer to complete the text. Then mark the letter (A), (B), (C), or (D) on your answer sheet.

Questions 131-134 refer to the following announcement.

We have now completed the installation of the new baggage carousels in Terminal 2. These devices ------- the baggage claim process by providing more areas for airlines to transfer the
131.
passengers' luggage. Also, with four new carousels of ------- sizes, Aircraft Ground Handling
132.
will be better able to cater to flights with high or low baggage loads. Above all, this ------- is
133.
an important step toward our airport's goal of offering outstanding customer service. -------.
134.
Josephine Perella is responsible for this process and will send an e-mail with complete details by this Friday.

131. (A) facilitate
 (B) will facilitate
 (C) were facilitating
 (D) have been facilitated

132. (A) differ
 (B) differs
 (C) differing
 (D) difference

133. (A) agreement
 (B) improvement
 (C) policy
 (D) insight

134. (A) All employees are required to receive training in the use of the new machines next week.
 (B) Regrettably, the cost of the carousels was higher than we had expected.
 (C) As you know, our business is very competitive nowadays.
 (D) Managers will be inspecting the new equipment later this week before deciding whether to make a purchase.

GO ON TO THE NEXT PAGE

Questions 135-138 refer to the following Web page.

www.sigamcmullenmarketing.com

Promoting your company is not a simple task. Traditional media outlets like newspapers and radio are ------- important marketing platforms, ------- advertising through online
    135.   **136.**
social media sites has become a lot more common nowadays. Siga McMullen Marketing specializes in both traditional and new media promotions. -------. In addition to an excellent
                                                                          137.
track record in traditional advertising, Siga McMullen Marketing also has the skills to -------
                                                                                        138.
your online presence. So don't delay! Call us today to benefit from our award-winning expertise.

135. (A) quickly
(B) even
(C) still
(D) close

136. (A) but
(B) rather
(C) then
(D) therefore

137. (A) Most marketing experts opt for TV commercials.
(B) We will create the most suitable campaign for your company.
(C) Old-fashioned advertising reaches more people.
(D) We have just updated our pricing policy.

138. (A) maximal
(B) maximum
(C) maximization
(D) maximize

Questions 139-142 refer to the following e-mail.

To: Magdalena Busto <mbusto@parkinginnovator.com>
From: Kevin Leoni <kleoni@investorscircle.com>
Date: April 2
Subject: ICC

Dear Ms. Busto,

This e-mail confirms receipt of your registration payment ------- (139.) verifies your status as an exhibitor at this year's Investor's Circle Conference (ICC) from June 13 to June 15. Since you registered more than two months in advance, you will be assigned a large booth at our ------- (140.) rate. Please note that this year, we are implementing a new requirement regarding booth usage. Now, all companies must have their booths cleared by 10:00 P.M. on the final day of the conference. ------- (141.). Recycling bins and trash cans will be provided. Thank you for taking part in this year's ------- (142.).

Sincerely,

Kevin Leoni, ICC Coordinator

139. (A) while
(B) instead of
(C) and also
(D) otherwise

140. (A) reduce
(B) reduced
(C) reduces
(D) reducing

141. (A) The number of investors attending is expected to be higher than ever this year.
(B) This means the complete removal of all materials including trash.
(C) The conference schedule will be released later this month.
(D) Your booth will be located adjacent to the West Exit, next to the hotel lobby.

142. (A) finding
(B) study
(C) election
(D) event

Questions 143-146 refer to the following article.

Concore Corporation Opens Manila Operations Center

Business News, New York (May 21) — Concore Corporation, a leading New York-based ------- of software programs, is expanding its operations overseas. This week, the firm
143.
opened its first operations center in the Philippines, in Manila. Since it was founded in 1972, Concore has been supplying software programs and data services to some of the world's largest financial organizations. -------. The majority of employees at the Manila facility will be
144.
hired locally. The company also hopes that up to 20 workers from the New York location will volunteer to relocate to Manila ------- the beginning of September, when the facility opens.
145.
But Concore spokesperson Jarvis Stanek emphasized that the Manila center represents an expansion, not relocation, of the company's operations, and that there will be no significant ------- in the number of New York staff.
146.

143. (A) developer
(B) developed
(C) develop
(D) development

144. (A) Data servers have become far more powerful.
(B) Several old buildings underwent renovations.
(C) A list of the company's major customers is available on its Web site.
(D) The opening for the position of operations manager has been filled.

145. (A) in spite of
(B) before
(C) so
(D) aside from

146. (A) opening
(B) applicant
(C) delay
(D) decrease

PART 7

Directions: In this part you will read a selection of texts, such as magazine and newspaper articles, e-mails, and instant messages. Each text or set of texts is followed by several questions. Select the best answer for each question and mark the letter (A), (B), (C), or (D) on your answer sheet.

Questions 147-148 refer to the following notice.

Next week, Weston Road will undergo surface repairs. For safety reasons, the Patterson Building's front doors will not be accessible from Monday, April 20, to Friday, April 25. Patterson staff members and clients are asked to use the back entrance on Windmill Avenue. Those who wish to go to the information desk should go through the back entrance and take the nearest elevator to the second floor.

147. Why was the notice posted?
   (A) To announce the renovation of a building
   (B) To explain some new safety regulations
   (C) To let employees know about an upcoming move
   (D) To advise of a temporary closure of an entrance

148. What is suggested about the Patterson Building?
   (A) It has both business and residential tenants.
   (B) Its main entryway is on Weston Road.
   (C) It will open again on Monday.
   (D) Its parking fees have increased.

GO ON TO THE NEXT PAGE

Questions 149-150 refer to the following e-mail.

From	Carl Schneider
To	Human Resources Department
Date	May 2
Subject	Safety training review

Hello all,

During the upcoming team meeting, our department will talk about ways to support new employees hired to work in our overseas plants. We want to ensure that every employee is thoroughly trained on all workplace safety procedures. To that end, each of you will need to prepare a presentation on three ways to ensure their knowledge rivals that of our domestic workers.

Best regards,

Carl Schneider
HR Director
Makalu Activewear, Inc.

149. According to the e-mail, what is suggested about Makalu Activewear, Inc.?

(A) It has a presence in other countries.
(B) It makes clothing from expensive materials.
(C) It will launch a new line of products.
(D) It has recently built a new factory.

150. What does Mr. Schneider ask the employees to do?

(A) Prepare to meet some clients
(B) Get ready for a meeting
(C) Review a new contract
(D) Attend an international conference

Questions 151-152 refer to the following information.

We at Smoctor Co. are known for producing top quality office furniture that can be easily assembled. We want to make sure that our customers are always satisfied with our products.

Before assembling your product, please confirm that all of the parts listed in the instructions are in the box.

If there are missing or damaged parts, do not return the item to the store from which you bought it. Instead, contact us directly to get replacement parts. Simply tell us what is missing or damaged, and we will send the new parts to you at no cost. To get in touch with us, call our toll-free number anytime at 1-888-494-4833, or email us at parts@smoctorco.com.

151. What is the purpose of the information?
(A) To give instructions on how to handle an issue regarding a purchase
(B) To provide customers with directions to a retail location
(C) To explain what customers can do to receive a complimentary gift
(D) To go over steps on how to assemble furniture

152. What is suggested about Smoctor Co.?
(A) It provides stores with replacement parts.
(B) Its user manuals can be downloaded online.
(C) It offers customer support at all times.
(D) Its members are eligible for free shipping.

GO ON TO THE NEXT PAGE

Questions 153-154 refer to the following online message chain.

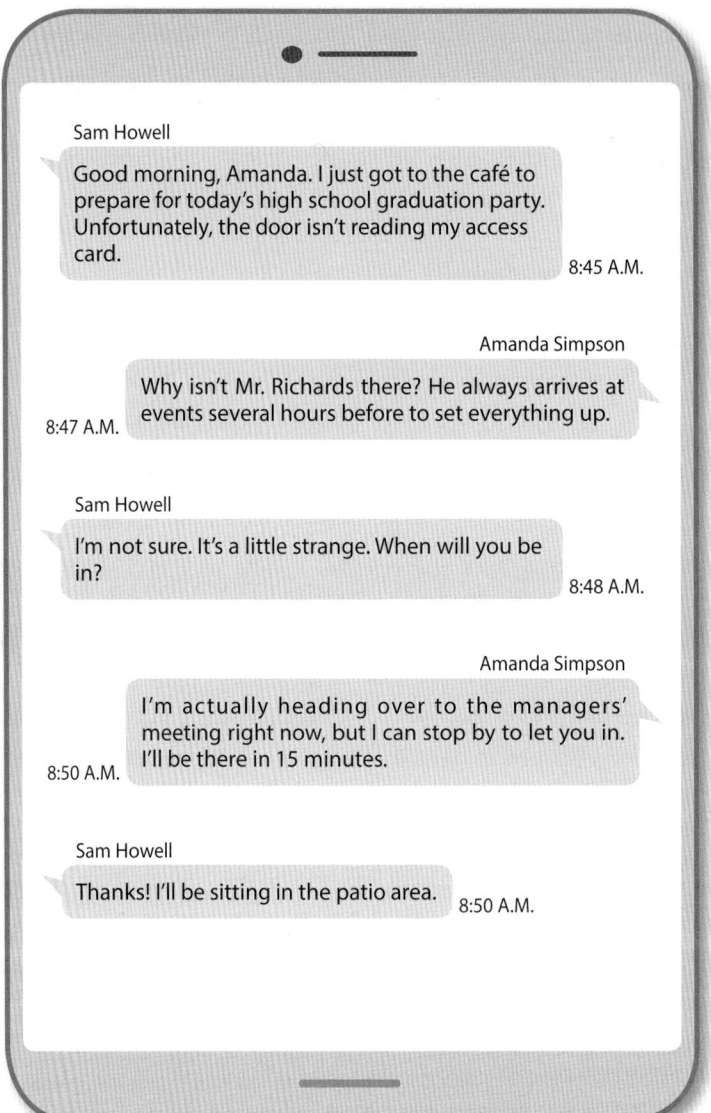

153. Who most likely is Ms. Simpson?

(A) A bakery owner
(B) A café manager
(C) A restaurant server
(D) A school administrator

154. At 8:48 A.M., what does Mr. Howell mean when he writes, "It's a little strange"?

(A) He brought a different access card.
(B) A course is not available.
(C) An employee normally comes in early.
(D) He does not have the correct documents.

Questions 155-157 refer to the following information from a brochure.

Planning a trip to Jackson City? Be sure to look for these popular spots!

Freemont State Park

The largest park in the state, Freemont State Park has facilities for camping, fishing, boating, and hiking. Admission is free. Park rangers are on duty 24 hours a day. Enjoy the outdoors and see the region's natural beauty.

Jackson City Aquarium

Open daily from 10 A.M. to 6 P.M. with a $10 admission fee. Children 12 and under get in free. Located by the harbor, the aquarium features more than 120 species of marine life. Daily dolphin and seal shows.

Jackson City Museum

Open Monday to Saturday from 9 A.M. to 5 P.M. with a $5 admission fee. Learn about the history of Jackson City and the surrounding region. Special exhibits alternate every other week.

Wakefield Gallery

Open Monday to Saturday from 9 A.M. to 6 P.M. No entrance fee, but financial contributions are always encouraged. Check out artwork from local artists as well as traveling exhibits from other galleries. Located beside the City Aquarium.

155. What is the purpose of the information?

(A) To provide details about tourist sites
(B) To promote a new business
(C) To list the achievements of a local artist
(D) To announce upcoming community events

156. What is indicated about the Jackson City Museum?

(A) It offers discounts to large groups.
(B) It regularly changes some of its exhibits.
(C) It does not charge admission for children.
(D) It closes earlier on weekends.

157. According to the information, what do the Jackson City Aquarium and the Wakefield Gallery have in common?

(A) Both are situated near water.
(B) Both charge for admission.
(C) Both provide audio tours.
(D) Both operate every day of the week.

GO ON TO THE NEXT PAGE

Questions 158-160 refer to the following article.

Murrayville Resident Wins Award
Wesley Smith, Staff Writer

December 8 – A resident of Murrayville was named Educator of the Year by the Organization of Professional Teachers (OPT). Fifty-four-year-old Georgia Weatherly received the award at the annual OPT banquet held in Omaha last night. According to OPT's latest press release, the award goes to "the candidate who has greatly contributed to enhancing the quality of education." OPT President Dr. Thomas Mandolin stated, "Ms. Weatherly has been working tirelessly in the education field for over 30 years." For the last 15 years, Ms. Weatherly has helped the OPT come up with innovative ways to keep students motivated in the classroom. Ms. Weatherly was born in Murrayville but went to school in Tulsa, where she started her career as a history teacher. She then returned to her hometown and joined Murrayville High School's faculty as a school counselor, and eventually worked her way up to her current position of principal. Ms. Weatherly is planning on running for superintendent of the Murrayville school district next year.

158. What is implied about Ms. Weatherly?

(A) She is a member of the OPT committee.
(B) She recently helped create a textbook.
(C) She helped raise educational standards.
(D) She plans to return to Tulsa in the future.

159. What happened 15 years ago?

(A) Ms. Weatherly started assisting the OPT.
(B) The OPT expanded its operations.
(C) Ms. Weatherly moved to Omaha.
(D) The OPT was established.

160. What was Ms. Weatherly's first job at Murrayville High School?

(A) School counselor
(B) History teacher
(C) Principal
(D) Superintendent

Questions 161-164 refer to the following notice.

NOTICE

Attn: All Managers
From: Westham Acres
Date: July 24

The California Public Water Company, our local water company, has told us that water levels in our area of the state are very low due to the lack of rain. For that reason, it is getting harder for them to satisfy the city's needs. Should water run out at the Westham Acres' property, we will have no choice but to shut down our facility.

The city council is requesting that all local businesses limit water use to avoid further problems. With this in mind, our facility will attempt to use less by turning off the sprinklers for all landscaping purposes and in some areas of the resort. In order to host the upcoming Westham Links Tournament, the fairway irrigation will continue to be run, but the lakes on the golf course will no longer be filled daily. Please help us by using sanitizer, rather than soap to clean your hands, to reduce personal water usage. Also, we will be changing the toilets to flush using 45 percent less water. When the plumbing crew arrives, please give them space to complete the renovations. Finally, all resort staff must continue to report for work, but landscaping crews will temporarily be placed on part-time schedules.

We appreciate your understanding in this matter.

161. The word "satisfy" in paragraph 1, line 3, is closest in meaning to

(A) fulfill
(B) please
(C) accomplish
(D) convince

162. What type of business is Westham Acres?

(A) A plumbing service
(B) A golf club
(C) A sporting goods store
(D) A water company

163. What are all staff members asked to do?

(A) Temporarily switch to a part-time schedule
(B) Finish their assignments ahead of time
(C) Revise the details of an upcoming event
(D) Allow plumbers to access to a work site

164. What does Westham Acres NOT plan to do to save water?

(A) Offer employees extra vacation days
(B) Stop filling some lakes every day
(C) Shut down the sprinklers
(D) Use hand sanitizer

Questions 165-167 refer to the following article.

Major Increases in Number of Visitors
By Eric O'Neil

White Mountain (January 15) — —[1]—. There was a significant number of visitors to resorts on White Mountain for the month of December. Compared to last December, 35 percent more people visited the White Mountain region.

These resorts have been reporting being at or near full occupancy for the past six weeks. —[2]—. This includes Gibraltar, the largest resort in the area with more than 500 rooms, and Pine Resort, which received guests for the first time on November 1 last year.

Anita Baker, Gibraltar's manager, commented, "We're definitely getting more reservations this year. Unlike last year, White Mountain has been getting a lot of snow. No slopes on White Mountain are closed like they were for part of the season last year." —[3]—. Ms. Baker added that due to the improving economy, people aren't afraid to spend more money on entertainment.

Hotels and resorts are not the only places benefitting from the increased spending. —[4]—. In addition, shops and restaurants in the towns around White Mountain are doing brisk business.

---

165. What is indicated about Pine Resort?

(A) It has been operating for a short period.
(B) It has more than 500 rooms.
(C) It is located at the bottom of White Mountain.
(D) It is attracting more customers than the Gibraltar Resort.

166. What is suggested about White Mountain?

(A) A ski tournament is held there annually.
(B) Several of its slopes are closed this year.
(C) It is the highest mountain in the country.
(D) It did not receive much snowfall last season.

167. In which of the positions marked [1], [2], [3], and [4] does the following sentence best belong?

"Local transportation companies are adding staff and vehicles to accommodate all the new demand."

(A) [1]
(B) [2]
(C) [3]
(D) [4]

Questions 168-171 refer to the following e-mail.

From	mike_burton@retailrenewals.com
To	zoe_cosse@jeansandmore.com
Subject	Store Analysis Review
Date	March 31

Dear Ms. Cosse,

—[1]—. I found that your store contained shelves packed with a wide array of clothing, but only a few signs to advertise your items. —[2]—. It is normal to want to offer customers as many options as possible, but visitors should, at a glance, be able to identify what your store's specialty is.

—[3]—. Many customer studies actually show that mall shoppers decide within just five seconds of entering a store whether they want to leave or stay and look around. That's why making an immediate impression is so important. —[4]—. In your store's displays, you should make it clear what you offer: casual clothing and accessories for teens and college students. I would recommend adding some pictures of models from this age group wearing your merchandise, along with some brief but appealing descriptions of what you offer. Racks and shelves should be simply organized to make it easy to find the featured items.

I certainly hope this is helpful information. If you would like your store to be redesigned as described, my company would be happy to work with you. When you called me several days ago, we discussed our rates. Now that I have seen the store, I can give you an exact price quote for the job. Please give me a call to set up an appointment.

Mike Burton
Retail Renewals

168. What problem with the store does Mr. Burton mention?

(A) It has many empty shelves.
(B) It does not have enough promotional materials.
(C) Some of the clothing items do not have price tags.
(D) The changing areas must be cleaned.

169. Why does Mr. Burton refer to customer studies?

(A) To describe a new method of payment
(B) To highlight future fashion trends
(C) To show how to feature a wide variety of clothing items
(D) To emphasize the importance of capturing guests' interest quickly

170. What is implied about Ms. Cosse?

(A) She helped Mr. Burton find some accessories.
(B) She has requested a discount for a service.
(C) She has many loyal customers.
(D) She talked with Mr. Burton over the phone.

171. In which of the positions marked [1], [2], [3], and [4] does the following sentence best belong?

"Per our discussion, I visited your business location yesterday."

(A) [1]
(B) [2]
(C) [3]
(D) [4]

Questions 172-175 refer to the following online chat discussion.

Tulsi Vembu [1:50 P.M.]
Hello, everyone. I would like to get a status update on the packaging materials for Oaktown Manufacturing.

James McKinney [1:52 P.M.]
We were initially supposed to deliver the boxes to their warehouse on Tuesday, but the blizzard has really pushed back our deliveries.

Tulsi Vembu [1:53 P.M.]
Is Oaktown aware of this?

Julie Tucker [1:55 P.M.]
I was planning to let them know, but I'm still waiting to hear from our drivers. James, are you able to help?

James McKinney [1:57 P.M.]
I just got off the phone with them. The roads are safe now, so they're departing soon. Everything should be delivered by Friday.

Julie Tucker [1:58 P.M.]
All right. I'll let them know that the shipment will arrive within the week.

James McKinney [2:00 P.M.]
At least we were able to ship out the boxes for Oaktown's scanners before the blizzard. We only have to send out the packaging materials for their printers now.

Tulsi Vembu [2:02 P.M.]
That's true, but we promised Oaktown that we would deliver packaging boxes for all of their items in a timely manner. We'll need to make sure to stick to this new schedule.

172. What kind of business do the writers most likely work for?

(A) An electronics manufacturer
(B) A packaging company
(C) A stationery store
(D) A catering service

173. What problem are the writers discussing?

(A) An order has been delayed.
(B) An item quantity was wrong.
(C) A payment has not been received.
(D) A driver is late to work.

174. What will Ms. Tucker most likely do next?

(A) Visit an office
(B) Get in touch with a client
(C) Purchase new supplies
(D) Review a legal document

175. At 1:55 P.M., what does Ms. Tucker mean when she writes, "are you able to help"?

(A) She believes a colleague should send an invoice.
(B) She would like a coworker to give an update.
(C) She needs to receive a manager's approval.
(D) She asks a supervisor to contact a customer.

GO ON TO THE NEXT PAGE

Questions 176-180 refer to the following flyer and e-mail.

The Swarsky Guild is preparing to begin its 37th year of providing the public with world-famous theatrical performances. This year, four historic plays as well as three contemporary dramas will be shown in Pretence Theater, located in downtown Akron, Ohio from April 5 to July 31.

The Swarsky Guild relies upon the generosity of corporate sponsors to be able to provide quality performances. To take advantage of our sponsor benefits or to receive a timetable of events, please call Lisa Merriweather at 555-9493.

The sponsorship levels along with their benefits are listed below:

Green Level – $1,000
Your firm's name will be put on our Web site, and your logo will be placed on the program that we sell at each performance.

Blue Level - $2,000
You will receive the same benefits as the Green Level and will also receive four season tickets for this year's performances.

Red Level - $5,000
In addition to receiving the same benefits as the Blue Level, members of your company who attend our season premiere performance will get a chance to meet the cast members after the show ends. Your company will also be thanked for being a sponsor at the start of each performance.

White Level - $10,000 and up
Along with all the benefits of the Red Level, your company's logo will be featured prominently in the theater's lobby before and after each performance as well as during intermission.

To	Greg Harper <gharper@boxen.com>
From	Tim Whittle <twhittle@swarskyguild.org>
Subject	Your Generosity
Date	February 24

Mr. Harper,

We at the Swarsky Guild are pleased that Boxen, Inc. sees the value in community theater. Your donation will help us to promote the theater arts to the public for another year.

We received your check for $2,000. Please send me a copy of your company's logo as soon as possible. On March 4, we will be printing the programs for the first play of the year, and we want to make sure your firm's logo appears in them. To express our appreciation for your continuing support of the Guild, I would like to offer Boxen the opportunity to meet with the cast after the initial performance at no additional cost. Four backstage tickets will be sent in addition to the sponsor passes.

Best,

Tim Whittle
President, Swarsky Guild

176. What is the purpose of the flyer?

(A) To encourage individuals to purchase season tickets
(B) To advertise the benefits of contributing to a group
(C) To give information about the history of an arts organization
(D) To provide a revised list of admission fees

177. According to the flyer, when should a call be placed to the Swarsky Guild?

(A) If tickets have not been delivered
(B) If a banking transaction is canceled
(C) If a schedule is needed
(D) If a company must cancel its financial contribution

178. What will happen on April 5?

(A) A banquet for the sponsors will be held.
(B) Some guests will meet cast members.
(C) City officials will attend a performance.
(D) A brand new theater will open in Akron.

179. What is suggested about the Swarsky Guild's performances?

(A) They are intended to encourage interest in the arts.
(B) They occur in multiple theaters during the year.
(C) They cannot be performed without several White Level sponsors.
(D) They have sold over 100 season passes so far.

180. What is NOT indicated about Boxen, Inc.?

(A) It will provide product demonstrations during intermissions.
(B) Its logo will be displayed in a performance program.
(C) It was a sponsor of Swarky Guild's events before.
(D) Its employees will meet some actors.

GO ON TO THE NEXT PAGE

Questions 181-185 refer to the following product reviews.

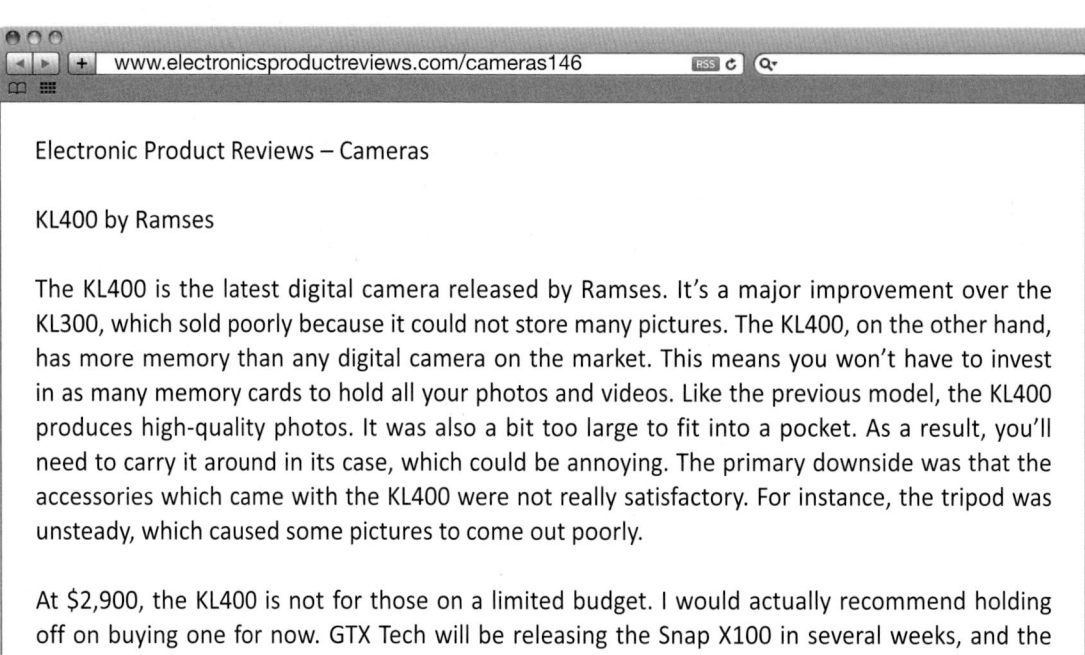

Electronic Product Reviews – Cameras

KL400 by Ramses

The KL400 is the latest digital camera released by Ramses. It's a major improvement over the KL300, which sold poorly because it could not store many pictures. The KL400, on the other hand, has more memory than any digital camera on the market. This means you won't have to invest in as many memory cards to hold all your photos and videos. Like the previous model, the KL400 produces high-quality photos. It was also a bit too large to fit into a pocket. As a result, you'll need to carry it around in its case, which could be annoying. The primary downside was that the accessories which came with the KL400 were not really satisfactory. For instance, the tripod was unsteady, which caused some pictures to come out poorly.

At $2,900, the KL400 is not for those on a limited budget. I would actually recommend holding off on buying one for now. GTX Tech will be releasing the Snap X100 in several weeks, and the KL400's price may drop in order to stay competitive.

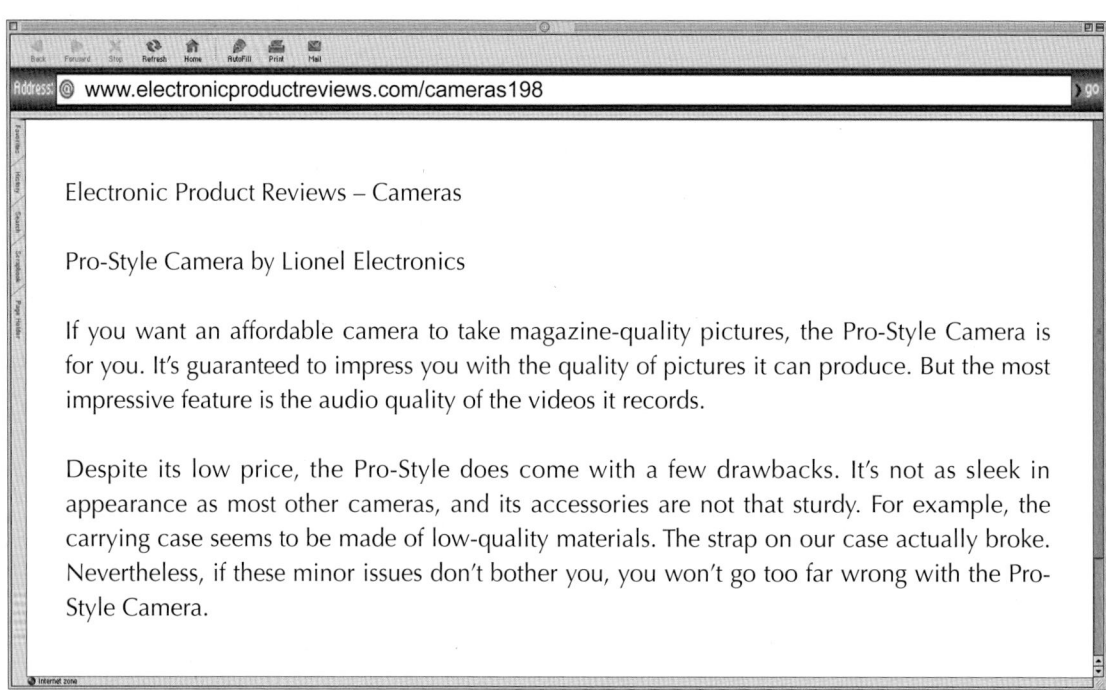

Electronic Product Reviews – Cameras

Pro-Style Camera by Lionel Electronics

If you want an affordable camera to take magazine-quality pictures, the Pro-Style Camera is for you. It's guaranteed to impress you with the quality of pictures it can produce. But the most impressive feature is the audio quality of the videos it records.

Despite its low price, the Pro-Style does come with a few drawbacks. It's not as sleek in appearance as most other cameras, and its accessories are not that sturdy. For example, the carrying case seems to be made of low-quality materials. The strap on our case actually broke. Nevertheless, if these minor issues don't bother you, you won't go too far wrong with the Pro-Style Camera.

181. What is suggested about Ramses?

(A) It has been in business for less than a year.
(B) It mostly manufactures affordable electronics.
(C) Its products are not always popular.
(D) Its items are manufactured overseas.

182. What is mentioned as a feature of the KL400?

(A) It can connect to the Internet.
(B) It comes with two different lenses.
(C) It has a large file capacity.
(D) It is more affordable than the Snap X100.

183. Why should customers hold off on purchasing the KL400?

(A) A new feature will be added.
(B) The lens will be improved.
(C) Its software will be updated.
(D) It will likely become cheaper.

184. What criticism did both cameras receive?

(A) Their accessories are not reliable.
(B) They sometimes take blurry photos.
(C) Their batteries do not last very long.
(D) They are not very portable.

185. According to the second review, what is the best feature of the Pro-Style Camera?

(A) It has a slim design.
(B) Its videos have good sound quality.
(C) Its settings are easy to configure.
(D) It is available in many colors.

Questions 186-190 refer to the following e-mails and addendum.

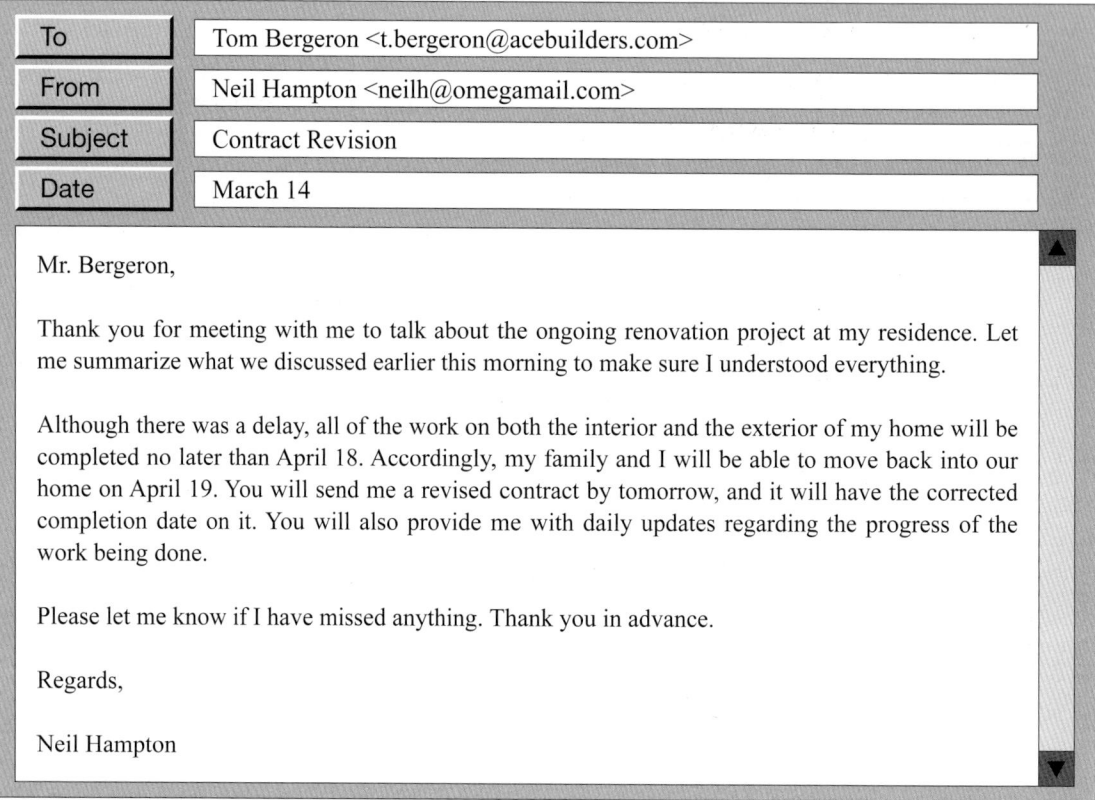

To	Tom Bergeron <t.bergeron@acebuilders.com>
From	Neil Hampton <neilh@omegamail.com>
Subject	Contract Revision
Date	March 14

Mr. Bergeron,

Thank you for meeting with me to talk about the ongoing renovation project at my residence. Let me summarize what we discussed earlier this morning to make sure I understood everything.

Although there was a delay, all of the work on both the interior and the exterior of my home will be completed no later than April 18. Accordingly, my family and I will be able to move back into our home on April 19. You will send me a revised contract by tomorrow, and it will have the corrected completion date on it. You will also provide me with daily updates regarding the progress of the work being done.

Please let me know if I have missed anything. Thank you in advance.

Regards,

Neil Hampton

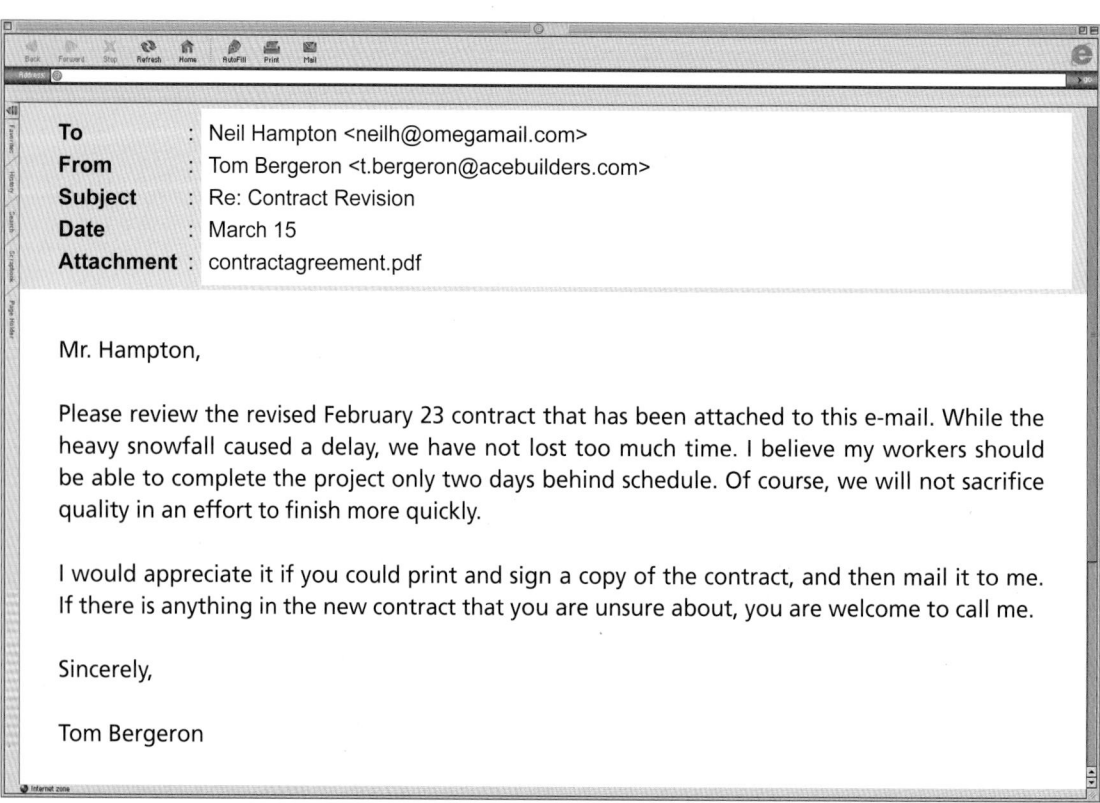

To	:	Neil Hampton <neilh@omegamail.com>
From	:	Tom Bergeron <t.bergeron@acebuilders.com>
Subject	:	Re: Contract Revision
Date	:	March 15
Attachment	:	contractagreement.pdf

Mr. Hampton,

Please review the revised February 23 contract that has been attached to this e-mail. While the heavy snowfall caused a delay, we have not lost too much time. I believe my workers should be able to complete the project only two days behind schedule. Of course, we will not sacrifice quality in an effort to finish more quickly.

I would appreciate it if you could print and sign a copy of the contract, and then mail it to me. If there is anything in the new contract that you are unsure about, you are welcome to call me.

Sincerely,

Tom Bergeron

Contract Addendum

Because of an emergency situation, no work was performed on the residence at 58 Mercury Lane on March 5 and March 6. As a result, the project's completion date has changed from April 16 to April 18. The home will be ready for move-in the following day. Ace Builders agrees to cover the cost of any extra charges during the last two days of the project.

Reports
Mr. Bergeron will provide Mr. Hampton with a progress report of the work that has been done every two days. These reports will be submitted by e-mail.

186. Who most likely is Mr. Hampton?

(A) A client of Mr. Bergeron
(B) A construction worker
(C) A coworker of Mr. Bergeron
(D) A real estate agent

187. What will happen on April 19?

(A) A project will be started.
(B) A residence will be occupied.
(C) A contract will be signed.
(D) A payment will be made.

188. In the second e-mail, the word "sacrifice" in paragraph 1, line 3, is closest in meaning to

(A) repeal
(B) consider
(C) neglect
(D) criticize

189. On what date was the work most likely delayed due to inclement weather?

(A) February 23
(B) March 5
(C) March 15
(D) April 16

190. What requested condition is NOT reflected in the contract addendum?

(A) The revised move-in day
(B) The frequency of progress reports
(C) The new completion date
(D) The payment of extra charges

GO ON TO THE NEXT PAGE

Questions 191-195 refer to the following article and e-mails.

Terraton to Get More Improvements

On Monday, the Terraton City Council held a meeting about future city projects. Since the renovation of the Terraton Public Library was completed under budget, the city has some surplus money. The council has created a list of several projects that could be financed with the left-over money.

Proposed projects include expansion of the playground at Terraton Elementary School, repair of the roads downtown, and addition of bicycle lanes to Ellsmire Avenue. Terraton Mayor Alicia Strauss stated that the council would like to hear the opinions of local residents regarding this matter. Residents can share their ideas at the next council meeting on Monday, June 11, at 6:30 P.M., or they can submit their suggestions by e-mail no later than June 16. Mayor Strauss said the final decision would be announced on June 28.

To	astrauss@terratoncitycouncil.org
From	tomchilders@elnet.com
Date	June 14
Subject	Project

Dear Mayor Strauss,

I would like to share my thoughts regarding how the city should spend the leftover funds. I regret I could not do so in person, but I went out of town for business on the day of the council meeting. I strongly believe the city should expand Terraton Elementary School's playground. The current play area is too small, and many parents have complained that their children do not have enough room to engage in recreational activities. My son is in the fifth grade, and he tells me that since the playground is so full, many students opt to just sit down and chat with friends. While this is not a bad alternative, I believe that children should utilize most of their break time engaging in physical activity. It is not healthy for elementary students to be inactive for long periods of time. Please seriously consider this suggestion for the sake of our children.

Regards,

Tom Childers

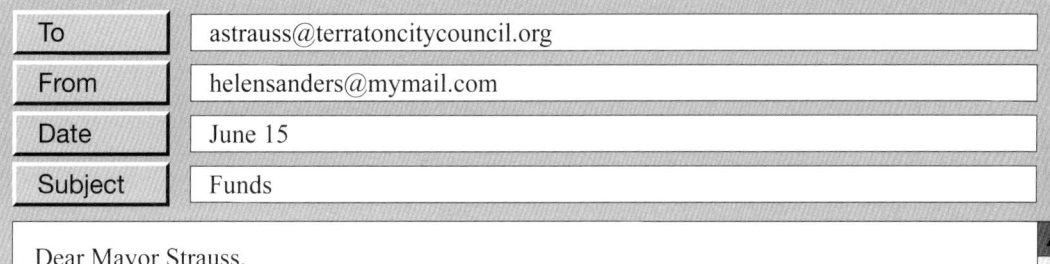

Dear Mayor Strauss,

It was great to hear the library was completed under budget. Too many projects these days exceed their budgets and wind up costing taxpayers even more money. I'm pleased that we seem to have a responsible government here in Terraton.

Now that we have a better library, it's only natural to fill it with as much material as possible. I propose purchasing more books and other educational materials for children with the remaining funds. With access to more resources, young students will be able to better increase their knowledge at an early age. Children are our future, and it is our responsibility to ensure that they have access to as many educational materials as possible.

Sincerely,

Helen Sanders

191. Why does Terraton have funds available?

(A) The city council raised taxes last month.
(B) Several residents have donated money.
(C) A recent project cost less than projected.
(D) A planned project was canceled.

192. When did Mr. Childers go on a business trip?

(A) On June 11
(B) On June 15
(C) On June 16
(D) On June 28

193. What does Mr. Childers indicate in his e-mail about the playground?

(A) It cannot accommodate many people.
(B) It should be near the library.
(C) It does not have safe equipment.
(D) It is far from the classrooms.

194. In the second e-mail, the word "natural" in paragraph 2, line 1, is closest in meaning to

(A) relaxing
(B) healthy
(C) reasonable
(D) plain

195. On what point would Mr. Childers and Ms. Sanders most likely agree?

(A) The city council should accept more suggestions from residents.
(B) The selected project should benefit a certain age group.
(C) The city should refund the surplus money to taxpayers.
(D) The funds should be split evenly between the school and the library.

Questions 196-200 refer to the following job advertisement, schedule, and e-mail.

Position: Professional Development Trainer
Location: Downtown Los Angeles

Hascom Energy, headquartered in the heart of downtown L.A., seeks a trainer to conduct a new computing class for our staff members at our in-house training facilities. The trainer must be available to teach a evening course (Monday to Friday) after the regular 9-to-6 working day. Class topic and focus will be set by the trainer. Pay is negotiable based on experience.

Email hiring@hascomenergy.com to apply, with the job position number 23934 in the subject line. A cover letter, résumé, and at least three references are required.

Hascom Energy
Los Angeles Headquarters

November Professional Training Schedule

The training facility operates between 7:00 A.M. and 9:00 P.M. weekdays. Registration for all classes isn't required, but certificates are only awarded to those who attend every class. All classes are held daily and last one month unless otherwise stated. The training facility uses rooms 701-713.

Course Title	Instructor	Time
Creating Presentations	Mark Cartwright	7:00 A.M. – 8:30 A.M. (MWF)
Database Management	Nadia Han	7:30 A.M. – 8:30 A.M.
Web Design	Dylan Brown	12:30 P.M. – 1:30 P.M. (MWF)
Software Programming	Alyssa Goldwater	7:45 P.M. – 8:45 P.M.

All Hascom Energy staff may sign up for the in-house training courses on the employee Web site. Employees from other branches may also take courses, but will need special permission from their managers.

From	Bianca Dumitrescu, Director of Personnel
To	Carmen McAllen, Professional Training Coordinator
Date	November 25
Subject	Re: New Professional Training Facility

I appreciated your thorough response to my inquiry about the new professional training courses. I'm really glad to hear that the courses are well-attended and that the new one that was just added is very popular. Some of our directors have called me, however, with some concerns. As you're aware, we give our employees a one-hour lunch break, but the lunchtime course is currently one hour long. This causes some workers to request more time to finish their meal, which sometimes leads to them completing their assignments later. It also creates issues when scheduling early afternoon meetings. Could this course be adjusted to run for only 40 minutes?

Thanks in advance; I appreciate the time and energy you have devoted to this project.

Bianca Dumitrescu
Director of Personnel
Hascom Energy

---

196. According to the job advertisement, what will the trainer determine?

(A) Where the course will take place
(B) What days the course is offered
(C) Which employees are eligible
(D) What course subject to teach

197. Who most likely is the newest professional trainer?

(A) Mr. Cartwright
(B) Ms. Han
(C) Mr. Brown
(D) Ms. Goldwater

198. What is indicated on the schedule?

(A) Staff from certain departments may take multiple courses.
(B) Staff from other company branches can use the training center.
(C) Staff may sign up one guest to attend class together.
(D) Staff may receive certifications after three months.

199. According to the e-mail, who contacted Ms. Dumitrescu over the telephone?

(A) A professional trainer
(B) A job applicant
(C) A corporate director
(D) A front-desk clerk

200. Which course will most likely be changed?

(A) Creating Presentations
(B) Database Management
(C) Web Design
(D) Software Programming

Stop! This is the end of the test. If you finish before time is called, you may go back to Part 5, 6, and 7 and check your work.

NO TEST MATERIAL ON THIS PAGE

NO TEST MATERIAL ON THIS PAGE

Answer Keys

MP3, 해석, 해설 온라인 무료 제공
모바일: QR코드 스캔을 통해 MP3 음원 바로 듣기 / 정답, 해석, 해설 바로 보기
PC: 파고다북스 사이트(www.pagodabook.com) 접속 / 로그인 후 다운로드

Listening Comprehension

1 (C)	2 (C)	3 (D)	4 (B)	5 (B)
6 (A)	7 (B)	8 (B)	9 (A)	10 (B)
11 (A)	12 (B)	13 (C)	14 (A)	15 (A)
16 (A)	17 (A)	18 (C)	19 (A)	20 (B)
21 (A)	22 (A)	23 (C)	24 (C)	25 (B)
26 (C)	27 (A)	28 (A)	29 (B)	30 (A)
31 (A)	32 (C)	33 (A)	34 (C)	35 (D)
36 (B)	37 (C)	38 (B)	39 (C)	40 (D)
41 (A)	42 (C)	43 (B)	44 (B)	45 (C)
46 (C)	47 (C)	48 (B)	49 (B)	50 (B)
51 (D)	52 (D)	53 (C)	54 (C)	55 (C)
56 (C)	57 (D)	58 (B)	59 (A)	60 (B)
61 (A)	62 (C)	63 (B)	64 (C)	65 (A)
66 (D)	67 (C)	68 (C)	69 (D)	70 (C)
71 (C)	72 (B)	73 (D)	74 (C)	75 (B)
76 (D)	77 (C)	78 (D)	79 (D)	80 (A)
81 (B)	82 (C)	83 (A)	84 (D)	85 (B)
86 (B)	87 (B)	88 (C)	89 (B)	90 (A)
91 (C)	92 (D)	93 (B)	94 (C)	95 (A)
96 (D)	97 (B)	98 (B)	99 (C)	100 (A)

Reading Comprehension

101 (C)	102 (B)	103 (A)	104 (A)	105 (A)
106 (A)	107 (D)	108 (B)	109 (C)	110 (A)
111 (D)	112 (A)	113 (B)	114 (C)	115 (B)
116 (D)	117 (B)	118 (B)	119 (D)	120 (B)
121 (B)	122 (D)	123 (A)	124 (A)	125 (B)
126 (C)	127 (C)	128 (A)	129 (D)	130 (B)
131 (B)	132 (C)	133 (B)	134 (A)	135 (C)
136 (A)	137 (B)	138 (D)	139 (C)	140 (B)
141 (B)	142 (D)	143 (A)	144 (C)	145 (B)
146 (D)	147 (D)	148 (B)	149 (A)	150 (B)
151 (A)	152 (C)	153 (B)	154 (C)	155 (A)
156 (B)	157 (A)	158 (C)	159 (A)	160 (A)
161 (A)	162 (B)	163 (D)	164 (A)	165 (A)
166 (D)	167 (D)	168 (B)	169 (D)	170 (D)
171 (A)	172 (B)	173 (A)	174 (B)	175 (B)
176 (B)	177 (C)	178 (B)	179 (A)	180 (A)
181 (C)	182 (C)	183 (D)	184 (A)	185 (B)
186 (A)	187 (B)	188 (C)	189 (B)	190 (B)
191 (C)	192 (A)	193 (A)	194 (C)	195 (B)
196 (D)	197 (D)	198 (B)	199 (C)	200 (C)

파고다토익 시험 직전 마무리 모의고사 TEST 2

초판 1쇄 인쇄 2017년 12월 27일
초판 1쇄 발행 2018년 1월 2일
초판 16쇄 발행 2024년 9월 30일

지 은 이 | 파고다교육그룹 언어교육연구소
펴 낸 이 | 박경실
펴 낸 곳 | PAGODA Books 파고다북스
출판등록 | 2005년 5월 27일 제 300-2005-90호
주　　소 | 06614 서울특별시 서초구 강남대로 419, 19층(서초동, 파고다타워)
전　　화 | (02) 6940-4070
팩　　스 | (02) 536-0660
홈페이지 | www.pagodabook.com

저작권자 | ⓒ 2018 파고다아카데미

이 책의 저작권은 저자와 출판사에 있습니다. 서면에 의한 저작권자와 출판사의 허락 없이
내용의 일부 혹은 전부를 인용 및 복제하거나 발췌하는 것을 금합니다.

Copyright ⓒ 2018 by PAGODA Academy

All rights reserved. No part of this publication may be reproduced, stored
in a retrieval system, or transmitted, in any form, or by any means, electronic,
mechanical, photocopying, recording or otherwise, without the prior written
permission of the copyright holder and the publisher.

ISBN 978-89-6281-808-6 (13740)

파고다북스　　www.pagodabook.com
파고다 어학원　www.pagoda21.com
파고다 인강　　www.pagodastar.com
테스트 클리닉　www.testclinic.com

| 낙장 및 파본은 구매처에서 교환해 드립니다.

PAGODA Books

파고다토익
시험 직전
마무리 TEST 3
모의고사

해설 바로 보기   음원 바로 듣기

PAGODA Books

시험 진행 안내

❶ **시험 시간: 120분(2시간)**
  · Listening Comprehension 100문제: 45분
  · Reading Comprehension 100문제: 75분
  · L/C 진행 후 휴식 시간 없이 바로 R/C 진행

❷ **준비물**
  · 컴퓨터용 사인펜 또는 연필

❸ **시험 응시 준수 사항**
  · 시험 시작 10분 전 입실 (이후에는 입실 불가)
  · 종료 30분 전과 10분 전에 시험 종료 공지함
  · 휴대전화의 전원을 꺼둘 것

❹ **OMR 답안지 표기 요령**
  · 반드시 컴퓨터용 사인펜 또는 연필로 표기
  · 개인정보, 문제번호, 단체명, 문제번호, 학과(부서) 및 학번코드 표기
   (학과(부서)코드는 별도 공지)

  ※ 개인정보, 문제번호, 학과(부서)코드, 주민등록번호를 틀리게 표기했을 경우 채점 및 성적
   확인이 불가능하므로 주의하시기 바랍니다.

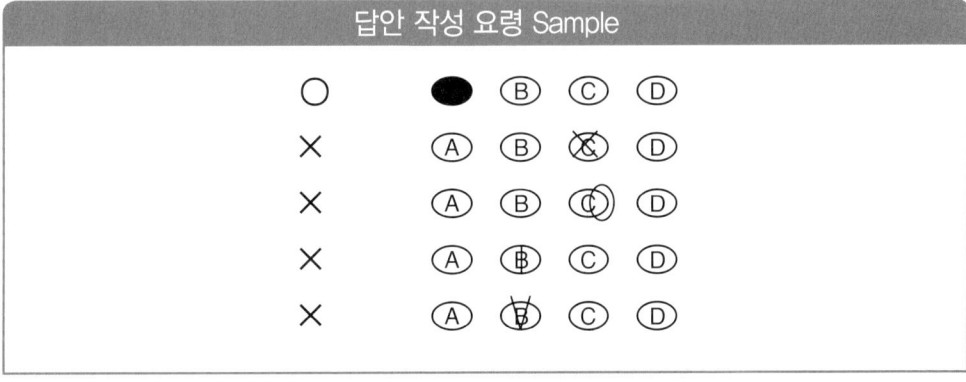

LISTENING TEST

In the Listening test, you will be asked to demonstrate how well you understand spoken English. The entire listening test will last approximately 45 minutes. There are four parts, and directions are given for each part. You must mark your answers on the separate answer sheet. Do not write your answers in your test book.

PART 1

Directions: For each question in this part, you will hear four statements about a picture in your test book. When you hear the statements, you must select the one statement that best describes what you see in the picture. Then find the number of the question on your answer sheet and mark your answer. The statements will not be printed in your test book and will be spoken only one time.

Statement (B), "A man is pointing at a document," is the best description of the picture, so you should select answer (B) and mark it on your answer sheet.

1.

2.

GO ON TO THE NEXT PAGE

3.

4.

5.

6.

GO ON TO THE NEXT PAGE

PART 2

Directions: You will hear a question or statement and three responses spoken in English. They will not be printed in your test book and will be spoken only one time. Select the best response to the question or statement and mark the letter (A), (B), or (C) on your answer sheet.

7. Mark your answer on your answer sheet.
8. Mark your answer on your answer sheet.
9. Mark your answer on your answer sheet.
10. Mark your answer on your answer sheet.
11. Mark your answer on your answer sheet.
12. Mark your answer on your answer sheet.
13. Mark your answer on your answer sheet.
14. Mark your answer on your answer sheet.
15. Mark your answer on your answer sheet.
16. Mark your answer on your answer sheet.
17. Mark your answer on your answer sheet.
18. Mark your answer on your answer sheet.
19. Mark your answer on your answer sheet.
20. Mark your answer on your answer sheet.
21. Mark your answer on your answer sheet.
22. Mark your answer on your answer sheet.
23. Mark your answer on your answer sheet.
24. Mark your answer on your answer sheet.
25. Mark your answer on your answer sheet.
26. Mark your answer on your answer sheet.
27. Mark your answer on your answer sheet.
28. Mark your answer on your answer sheet.
29. Mark your answer on your answer sheet.
30. Mark your answer on your answer sheet.
31. Mark your answer on your answer sheet.

PART 3

Directions: You will hear some conversations between two or more people. You will be asked to answer three questions about what the speakers say in each conversation. Select the best response to each question and mark the letter (A), (B), (C), or (D) on your answer sheet. The conversations will not be printed in your test book and will be spoken only one time.

32. Where most likely are the speakers?
    (A) At an art gallery
    (B) At a concert hall
    (C) At a movie theater
    (D) At a train station

33. Why does the man apologize to the woman?
    (A) A venue is closed.
    (B) Some fees have gone up.
    (C) A performance has been rescheduled.
    (D) Some tickets are not available.

34. What will the woman probably do next?
    (A) Call a taxi
    (B) Fill out a survey
    (C) Get a membership
    (D) Sign up for a tour

35. Why does the woman say, "I still don't have our projected expenses"?
    (A) She requires more time to finish a task.
    (B) She needs a document from the man.
    (C) She would like to explain a mistake.
    (D) She wants to reschedule a meeting with the man.

36. What does the man say about the staffing cost?
    (A) It will be difficult to calculate.
    (B) It was missing some information.
    (C) It will be higher than anticipated.
    (D) It was not approved on time.

37. What will the woman talk about at a meeting?
    (A) A staff directory
    (B) A training workshop
    (C) An employee evaluation
    (D) A hiring option

38. What is the man responsible for doing?
    (A) Arranging a client meeting
    (B) Hosting a company tour
    (C) Installing some software
    (D) Training new employees

39. Where most likely do the speakers work?
    (A) At a factory
    (B) At a hospital
    (C) At a catering company
    (D) At an accounting firm

40. What does the man say he will do?
    (A) Check some computers
    (B) Get a replacement presenter
    (C) Pick up some food
    (D) Make a room reservation

41. What are the speakers mainly discussing?
    (A) Changing a manufacturing procedure
    (B) Designing a new company logo
    (C) Preparing for an upcoming convention
    (D) Recommending a candidate for an award

42. What does the woman suggest?
    (A) Hiring a consultant
    (B) Creating a brochure
    (C) Adjusting a schedule
    (D) Distributing a survey

43. What is Joseph concerned about?
    (A) A broken machine
    (B) A missing document
    (C) A tight deadline
    (D) A customer complaint

GO ON TO THE NEXT PAGE

44. What does the man want to know?

 (A) How much an item costs
 (B) Where a display is located
 (C) How long a sale lasts
 (D) What sizes are available

45. Why does the man say, "This backpack is really nice"?

 (A) To get a discount from an employee
 (B) To request permission to try on a bag
 (C) To show appreciation for a gift
 (D) To express interest in buying a product

46. What will the woman most likely do next?

 (A) Exchange some merchandise
 (B) Bring a coupon
 (C) Contact another store
 (D) Search a system

47. What kind of business do the speakers most likely work for?

 (A) A flower distributor
 (B) A catering service
 (C) An auto parts warehouse
 (D) A furniture manufacturing company

48. What problem does the woman mention?

 (A) A tool malfunctioned.
 (B) A cost increased.
 (C) A worker was unavailable.
 (D) A package was damaged.

49. What does the woman say will happen?

 (A) A technician will repair a machine.
 (B) An order will be prepared on time.
 (C) A customer will receive a refund.
 (D) A business will be open late.

50. Why is the man worried?

 (A) A shipment is late.
 (B) Sales have been poor.
 (C) Inclement weather is expected.
 (D) Transportation fees have increased.

51. What will the woman decide tomorrow?

 (A) When to start a promotion
 (B) When to meet with clients
 (C) Whether an order should be canceled
 (D) Whether a business will open

52. What does the man offer to do?

 (A) Lead a training session
 (B) Notify coworkers
 (C) Pick up a package
 (D) Display some products

53. Where does the conversation most likely take place?

 (A) At an airline service counter
 (B) At a car rental agency
 (C) At a hotel reception desk
 (D) At a baggage claim area

54. What does the man say the women will receive?

 (A) A map
 (B) A product catalog
 (C) A voucher
 (D) A seat upgrade

55. What will the women probably do next?

 (A) Attend a conference
 (B) Send an e-mail
 (C) Have a meal
 (D) Contact a coworker

56. Why did the woman contact the man?

(A) To request a revised invoice
(B) To provide new contact information
(C) To find out how to use a product
(D) To inquire about a delivery status

57. According to the man, what was the problem?

(A) An incorrect address was given.
(B) A discount was not applied.
(C) A phone line was busy.
(D) An office was not open.

58. What does the man say he will do for the woman?

(A) Refund a charge
(B) Send a manual
(C) Replace an item
(D) Speak with a customer

59. Where most likely is the conversation taking place?

(A) At a parking lot
(B) In an electronics store
(C) At an auto shop
(D) In an office building

60. What does the woman say she will do?

(A) Pay a fee online
(B) Rent a car
(C) Come back tomorrow
(D) Get some cash

61. What will be sent to the woman?

(A) A revised invoice
(B) A discount coupon
(C) A card number
(D) A text message

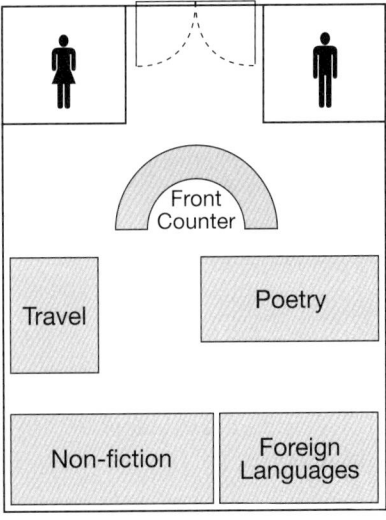

62. What most likely is the woman's occupation?

(A) Library clerk
(B) University professor
(C) Novel writer
(D) Sales associate

63. What does the man say about the book?

(A) It is being sold at a reduced price.
(B) It can be ordered through a Web site.
(C) It is popular in other countries.
(D) It contains many discussion topics.

64. Look at the graphic. Where is the book that the man is looking for located?

(A) In the Travel section
(B) In the Poetry section
(C) In the Non-fiction section
(D) In the Foreign Languages section

GO ON TO THE NEXT PAGE

Rating (Out of 5): The Harborside Café

Comfort: 4

Pricing: 3

Guest Services: 5

Dish Selections: 2

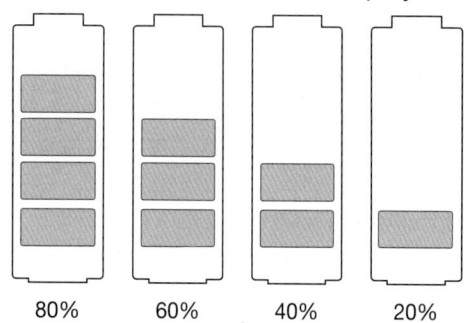

65. Who is the woman?

   (A) A magazine journalist
   (B) A head chef
   (C) A restaurant manager
   (D) A food critic

66. Look at the graphic. What area does the man say needs to be improved?

   (A) Comfort
   (B) Pricing
   (C) Guest Services
   (D) Dish Selections

67. What suggestion does the woman make?

   (A) Conducting a survey
   (B) Remodeling an area
   (C) Speaking with employees
   (D) Lowering some prices

68. What is taking place?

   (A) A technology conference
   (B) A safety inspection
   (C) A training workshop
   (D) A building tour

69. What does the woman ask about?

   (A) The number of guests
   (B) A manufacturing process
   (C) The size of a device
   (D) A backup power source

70. Look at the graphic. According to the man, how many bars will be displayed when the battery should be replaced?

   (A) One bar
   (B) Two bars
   (C) Three bars
   (D) Four bars

PART 4

Directions: You will hear some talks given by a single speaker. You will be asked to answer three questions about what the speaker says in each talk. Select the best response to each question and mark the letter (A), (B), (C), or (D) on your answer sheet. The talks will not be printed in your test book and will be spoken only one time.

71. What is the broadcast mainly about?

    (A) A traffic report
    (B) A weather forecast
    (C) A construction project
    (D) A national holiday

72. What does the speaker say will begin tomorrow?

    (A) A sports event
    (B) A musical performance
    (C) An annual conference
    (D) A food festival

73. What does the speaker suggest doing?

    (A) Sharing cars
    (B) Checking a Web site
    (C) Using public transportation
    (D) Taking an umbrella

74. Where most likely is the announcement being made?

    (A) At a community center
    (B) At a manufacturing facility
    (C) At a hotel banquet hall
    (D) At a department store

75. According to the speaker, what will happen at the end of the event?

    (A) A book signing will be held.
    (B) A winner will be announced.
    (C) People will take photos.
    (D) Experts will offer advice.

76. What is said about Retro Rack?

    (A) It has received positive reviews.
    (B) It has just opened for business.
    (C) It is offering free food.
    (D) It is moving to a new location.

77. Where is the speaker most likely calling?

    (A) A convention center
    (B) A moving company
    (C) An auto service center
    (D) A public transportation company

78. Why did the speaker take the subway?

    (A) His bus didn't arrive.
    (B) His car wasn't working.
    (C) He was feeling sick.
    (D) He was unsure about a location.

79. What does the speaker want to know?

    (A) When an event will start
    (B) Whether a schedule has changed
    (C) How to use a Web site
    (D) How much a fee will be

80. What probably is the speaker's job?

    (A) Product designer
    (B) Staffing manager
    (C) Factory supervisor
    (D) Tour guide

81. What does the speaker mean when he says, "the submission deadline was June 10"?

    (A) A report was submitted.
    (B) A task must proceed.
    (C) A date should be checked.
    (D) A position has been filled.

82. What does the speaker say will happen later this week?

    (A) A facility will be inspected.
    (B) A product will be launched.
    (C) Some interviews will be held.
    (D) Some fees will be reduced.

GO ON TO THE NEXT PAGE

83. According to the speaker, what did the *Stonetown Gazette* recently do?

(A) It promoted an event.
(B) It lowered its prices.
(C) It hired an accounting firm.
(D) It rated some companies.

84. What does the speaker imply when she says, "a major accounting firm will soon be opening an office in our area"?

(A) There will be more competition for business.
(B) An organization will be audited.
(C) There will be job opportunities for people.
(D) A facility will be renovated.

85. What does the speaker say her company has bought?

(A) An office building
(B) A computer program
(C) A magazine subscription
(D) A delivery truck

86. What is Simply Connect?

(A) A laptop computer
(B) A building security system
(C) A mobile phone
(D) A teleconferencing program

87. What does the speaker mean when she says, "Don't you have more important things to do"?

(A) Other systems are inefficient.
(B) Meetings take too much time.
(C) Personal calls should not be made.
(D) Employee training must be improved.

88. According to the speaker, why should listeners visit a Web site?

(A) To download a voucher
(B) To sign up for a class
(C) To place an order
(D) To learn about a product

89. What change is being discussed?

(A) How office supplies are purchased
(B) How customer data is stored
(C) How products are monitored
(D) How equipment is used

90. What does the speaker say the company will be able to do?

(A) Hire more employees
(B) Shorten delivery times
(C) Provide discounted prices
(D) Open overseas branches

91. Why will Ms. Hwang be visiting the company?

(A) To train staff
(B) To repair computers
(C) To inspect merchandise
(D) To conduct interviews

92. What type of business does the man most likely work for?

(A) A real estate agency
(B) A business consulting firm
(C) An interior design store
(D) A tour operating company

93. What problem does the man mention?

(A) An office is not big enough.
(B) A price may be too high.
(C) A deadline has passed.
(D) A seat is not available.

94. What does the man ask the listener to do by the end of the day?

(A) Send him a payment
(B) Make a decision
(C) Check an advertisement
(D) Revise a document

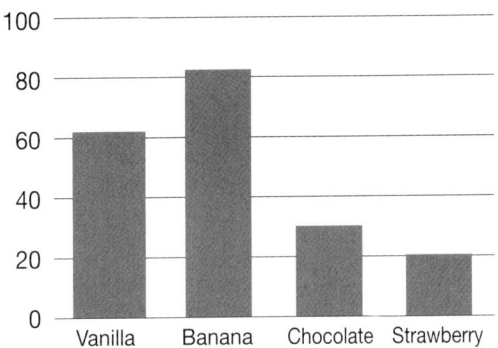

95. Look at the graphic. Which cake will be discounted this month?

(A) Vanilla
(B) Banana
(C) Chocolate
(D) Strawberry

96. Why does the speaker thank Nikolai?

(A) He created a new kind of cake.
(B) He analyzed some sales figures.
(C) He suggested a promotional event.
(D) He offered to work on the weekend.

97. What are the listeners encouraged to do?

(A) Share ideas
(B) Try sample products
(C) Invite some guests
(D) Enter a contest

98. Where does the speaker work?

(A) At a library
(B) At a car rental agency
(C) At a bank
(D) At a utility company

99. Look at the graphic. How much late fee has been charged to the listener?

(A) $5
(B) $10
(C) $15
(D) $20

100. What should the listener provide to sign up for a service?

(A) A home address
(B) A driver's license
(C) Some phone numbers
(D) Some payment information

This is the end of the Listening test. Turn to Part 5 in your test book.

GO ON TO THE NEXT PAGE

READING TEST

In the Reading test, you will read a variety of texts and answer several different types of reading comprehension questions. The entire Reading test will last 75 minutes. There are three parts, and directions are given for each part. You are encouraged to answer as many questions as possible within the time allowed.

You must mark your answers on the separate answer sheet. Do not write your answers in your test book.

PART 5

Directions: A word or phrase is missing in each of the sentences below. Four answer choices are given below each sentence. Select the best answer to complete the sentence. Then mark the letter (A), (B), (C), or (D) on your answer sheet.

101. With this application, you can ------- with coworkers and colleagues wherever they may be.

    (A) communicate
    (B) express
    (C) inform
    (D) arrive

102. Access to Sonrato County Bridge will be restricted over the next two weeks ------- renovation work on several lanes.

    (A) as a consequence
    (B) because of
    (C) according to
    (D) provided that

103. ------- that large accounting contract was an impressive accomplishment for the small financial firm.

    (A) Had secured
    (B) Securing
    (C) Secure
    (D) Secures

104. The drama's first episode was rescheduled, and it is now going to be broadcast next Friday -------.

    (A) instead
    (B) again
    (C) always
    (D) often

105. After conducting Mr. Pedro's final interview, the CEO ------- the IT director's decision to promote him to Senior Systems Analyst.

    (A) produced
    (B) gathered
    (C) finalized
    (D) invited

106. Vice President Hemsley has extensive background in marketing and so has appointed ------- to fill the vacant marketing director position.

    (A) he
    (B) him
    (C) himself
    (D) his

107. ------- needs to be determined is the venue for the company's upcoming anniversary banquet.

    (A) Whichever
    (B) Whose
    (C) Which
    (D) What

108. Laboratory tests show that the fabric could not ------- have been stained by our detergent.

    (A) possibilities
    (B) possibility
    (C) possible
    (D) possibly

109. The sales director expressed his faith in Harfager, Inc.'s ------- to complete the initiative on time.

(A) trouble
(B) ability
(C) trust
(D) desire

110. Architects should make ------- estimates of material and labor costs to avoid disputes when finalizing the quote.

(A) temporary
(B) eager
(C) accurate
(D) stringent

111. Parfum, Inc.'s directors are ------- a new line of cosmetics for male customers in their thirties.

(A) considers
(B) consider
(C) considered
(D) considering

112. Reducing food intake can often be effective for weight loss, although not ------- good for your health.

(A) permanently
(B) suspiciously
(C) accordingly
(D) necessarily

113. What customers like best ------- shopping at GH Department Store is the attentive staff.

(A) against
(B) seeing
(C) about
(D) toward

114. Items that are purchased in this store are not ------- without the original receipt.

(A) exchanging
(B) exchange
(C) exchanges
(D) exchangeable

115. Although renovation of the manufacturing plant is not ------- completed, most of the machines are back in operation.

(A) quite
(B) seldom
(C) ever
(D) a lot

116. Gravesend Packaging Solutions and Carentan Electronics have signed a new contract with -------.

(A) they
(B) oneself
(C) themselves
(D) each other

117. Our writers produce a good number of articles ------- tight deadlines.

(A) until
(B) within
(C) upon
(D) into

118. As they did with the first, event coordinators of the Stanon Entrepreneurs' Conference ------- were able to find a replacement for the second canceled lecture.

(A) more
(B) thereafter
(C) likewise
(D) very

119. Gateway Properties has put a golf course up for sale, ------- the large area of undeveloped land that runs alongside it.

(A) though
(B) along with
(C) while
(D) regardless of

120. Since Darden's new smartphone is set ------- soon, our store can start advertising the product.

(A) will have launched
(B) launching
(C) launched
(D) to launch

GO ON TO THE NEXT PAGE

121. To check your current ------- status, log on to the Student Account section of the Harjav College Web site.

    (A) disclaimer
    (B) stock
    (C) agreement
    (D) enrollment

122. If Ms. Crichek had remained with company longer, she ------- the employee manual.

    (A) had been revising
    (B) revises
    (C) could have revised
    (D) will revise

123. Despite performing ------- analysis, the engineers were unable to determine the cause of the problem with the new solar panel.

    (A) exhaust
    (B) exhausted
    (C) exhaustedly
    (D) exhaustive

124. The museum ------- has attracted a large number of visitors over the weekend.

    (A) opening
    (B) opened
    (C) opens
    (D) open

125. Applications for the ------- position on our management team must be received by next Monday.

    (A) unavailable
    (B) unfilled
    (C) unqualified
    (D) unwanted

126. Ms. Doyen's comments are in regard to the e-mail and memo dated 11 and 14, October, -------.

    (A) respecting
    (B) respective
    (C) respectively
    (D) respects

127. PGD Group has ------- as the leading institute in the field of foreign language education.

    (A) emerged
    (B) displayed
    (C) produced
    (D) appointed

128. Drivers still need to signal when they make a turn ------- there are no other cars around.

    (A) for instance
    (B) even if
    (C) nevertheless
    (D) unless

129. Ms. Kim ------- authority to the most experienced staff member in her store while she was away.

    (A) operated
    (B) delegated
    (C) submitted
    (D) aligned

130. The latest survey shows that the ------- of RW's new automobile were far more significant than its benefits.

    (A) compliments
    (B) disturbances
    (C) credits
    (D) shortcomings

PART 6

Directions: Read the texts that follow. A word, phrase, or sentence is missing in parts of each text. Four answer choices for each question are given below the text. Select the best answer to complete the text. Then mark the letter (A), (B), (C), or (D) on your answer sheet.

Questions 131-134 refer to the following article.

Willa International Corporation Announces Purchase of Genil Technologies

Taipei — Willa International Corporation (WIC) confirmed Monday that ------- plans to
131.
purchase Genil Technologies for $300 million.

A WIC spokesperson said that the acquisition would enable the company to increase production. WIC has started accepting much larger orders since it will soon have exclusive use of Genil Technologies' state-of-the-art factories. -------.
132.

According to industry experts, the purchase of Genil Technologies will give WIC the highest production volume for circuits of any company in the business. "It will move far ahead of the
-------," leading analyst Marvin White said.
133.

WIC says it has no plans to reduce Genil Technologies' workforce. -------, it may hire
134.
new employees to cope with the rising demand it predicts for smartphone components worldwide in the years to come.

131. (A) someone
 (B) it
 (C) she
 (D) these

132. (A) All the plants are expected to be operating at full capacity.
 (B) Plans to buy other companies were unsuccessful.
 (C) Further acquisitions will be made later this year.
 (D) The deal will increase employee satisfaction.

133. (A) competition
 (B) deadline
 (C) contract
 (D) delivery

134. (A) Consequently
 (B) Rather
 (C) Similarly
 (D) Still

GO ON TO THE NEXT PAGE

Questions 135-138 refer to the following notice.

The Segovia Hotel: Bookings

Since the availability of accommodations in Segovia is severely ------- during the summer
135.
months, we recommend booking in advance at this time of year. A single-night deposit is
required in order to reserve a room. Deposits ------- in full if cancellations are made one
136.
week before the scheduled check-in date. In the event that a booking is canceled within
seven days of the arrival date, the full charge for the whole ------- will be billed to the
137.
customer. -------.
138.

135. (A) limit
(B) limits
(C) limited
(D) limitations

136. (A) were returned
(B) will be returned
(C) had been returning
(D) are returning

137. (A) stay
(B) week
(C) party
(D) extension

138. (A) All hotel guests have access to free wireless internet.
(B) Furthermore, we will be opening another hotel in Segovia later this year.
(C) Early departures will also be subject to these terms.
(D) We hope that you were happy with the service provided.

Questions 139-142 refer to the following notice.

Approval for New Tablets

New tools for instruction ------- to the schools of Farnley. Lorna Turner, President of the
139.
Farnley Board of Education, announced that an educational technology program proposed

to the city government last month has been approved. -------.
140.

The initiative makes $40,000 available to every school in Farnley to order tablet PCs.

Students will usually be required to keep their tablets at school for use ------- school hours,
141.
though exceptions will be made when special ------- or projects require the devices to be
142.
used at home.

139. (A) were coming
(B) are coming
(C) come
(D) came

140. (A) However, the president is happy with the result.
(B) The device will be made available at a low price.
(C) Fortunately, the final decision is expected soon.
(D) City authorities voted on the proposal last Wednesday.

141. (A) on
(B) during
(C) to
(D) from

142. (A) charges
(B) grades
(C) assignments
(D) measures

GO ON TO THE NEXT PAGE

Questions 143-146 refer to the following letter.

June 24

Oliver Lemar
Canelam Industries
1644 Yellow Hill Road
Springdale, AR 72764

Dear Mr. Lemar,

Thank you for ordering 30 toner cartridges from Lawson Copier Supplies. We have processed your payment, and your order has been prepared for shipping. -------. **143.**

We realize that you previously used a different supplier and decided to make the switch to Lawson Copier Supplies. We are delighted that you have chosen us for your company's printing supply needs, and we are applying a 10 percent discount to this ------- order to **144.** show our appreciation. -------, we are waiving your shipping fee. Please find enclosed your **145.** revised invoice and a check for $12.99.

Thank you for ------- Lawson Copier Supplies. We appreciate the opportunity and look **146.** forward to serving you for many years to come.

Sincerely,

Jian Chao
Customer Service Manager

Enclosures

143. (A) We are truly grateful for the opportunity to earn your business for so many years.
(B) Delivery will be made to you in 3–5 working days.
(C) However, you appear to have paid too much.
(D) Regrettably, we are currently out of the items you ordered.

144. (A) first
(B) partial
(C) future
(D) recurring

145. (A) Yet
(B) Nevertheless
(C) For instance
(D) Moreover

146. (A) chooses
(B) choosing
(C) to choose
(D) chosen

PART 7

Directions: In this part you will read a selection of texts, such as magazine and newspaper articles, e-mails, and instant messages. Each text or set of texts is followed by several questions. Select the best answer for each question and mark the letter (A), (B), (C), or (D) on your answer sheet.

Questions 147-148 refer to the following receipt.

Receipt Number: 950590-34843
(Please make a note of this receipt number. You may need it if you require assistance from Customer Service.)

Received by Maurice Davidson: $70 payment made to Delmont Theater
Paid for by credit card (Last four digits: 3920)

Description: Two tickets for the Harborville Orchestra performance on Saturday, August 17, at 8:00 P.M.

NOTE: Print this receipt and bring it to the theater. You will not be sent a receipt in the mail. Present this receipt at the box office before the performance begins in order to collect your tickets. All sales are final.

147. What does Mr. Davidson intend to do on August 17?

(A) Make a payment
(B) Watch a show
(C) Apply for a reimbursement
(D) Contact customer service

148. What should Mr. Davidson bring with him?

(A) A credit card
(B) A receipt
(C) A ticket
(D) A photo ID

GO ON TO THE NEXT PAGE

Questions 149-151 refer to the following invoice.

INVOICE

From: Hanover, Inc.
534 W. Main St.
Seattle, WA 98101

Billed To: Russell Wainwright, Carter Legal Partners
Ship To (on November 10): Carter Legal Partners
Landover Road, Walla Walla, WA 99362

Item Code	Description	Quantity
KE373	Leather Chair	8
P0958	Oak Desk	8
MM432	Cubicle Partition	14
WH382*	Conference Table	1

*Item #WH382 is currently unavailable at our warehouse. It will be specially ordered and delivered on a later date than the other items.

---

149. What type of business most likely is Hanover, Inc.?

(A) An office furniture store
(B) An interior design firm
(C) A delivery service
(D) A law office

150. What will probably happen on November 10?

(A) A refund will be processed.
(B) An order will be sent.
(C) A bill will be updated.
(D) A purchase will be made.

151. What is indicated about the table?

(A) It is currently not in stock.
(B) It is being sold at a reduced price.
(C) It will arrive before the other items.
(D) It will be discontinued soon.

Questions 152-153 refer to the following text message.

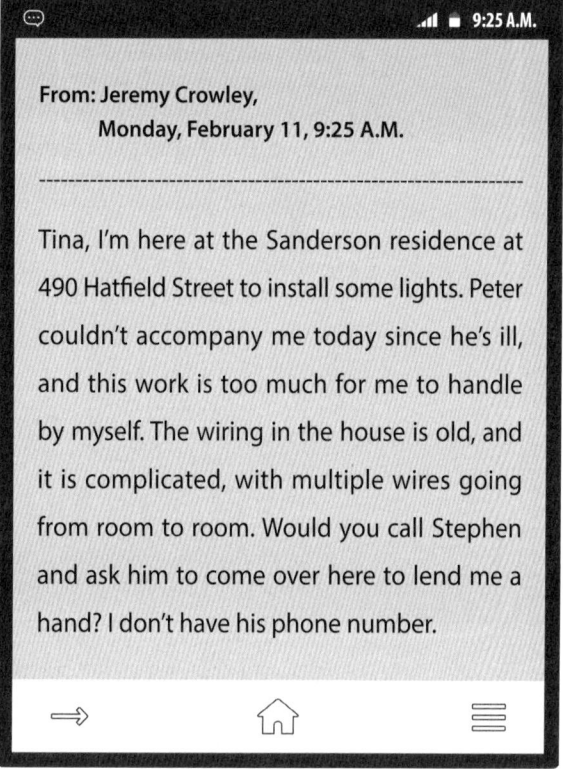

152. What problem does Mr. Crowley have?

(A) He has never installed lights before.
(B) He is sick and has to go home.
(C) He cannot complete a project alone.
(D) He needs directions to a residence.

153. Why did Mr. Crowley send the text message to Tina?

(A) To have her contact a coworker
(B) To ask for an address
(C) To tell her to send him a number
(D) To find out where Peter is working

Questions 154-155 refer to the following survey.

The Montpelier Hotel

Thank you for staying at The Montpelier Hotel. We strive to provide the best service for our guests. We would love to hear from you regarding how we are doing. We would appreciate it if you completed this short form, and then left it at the front desk during your checkout.

How did you enjoy your stay at The Montpelier Hotel?

Please rate the following categories:

Category	Very Satisfied	Satisfied	Not Satisfied
Customer Service		V	
Cleanliness	V		
Interior	V		
Dining Service		V	

Would you recommend The Montpelier Hotel to friends?   Yes   No

Please provide any other feedback in the space below.

I love how the hotel looks now that you have renovated it. It's also much cleaner than it was before. Overall, the service is good, but there were several times where the housekeeping staff cleaned my room late. I also thought the food at the hotel's restaurant could have been better.

May we contact you for more information? If you agree to this request, please leave your name and phone number below.

Christopher Kilgore
(893) 532-8574

154. What are guests encouraged to do?

(A) Post an online review
(B) Make an advance payment
(C) Visit a gift shop
(D) Submit a form

155. What is suggested about Mr. Kilgore?

(A) He stayed at the hotel for the first time.
(B) He will talk to a hotel worker about his stay.
(C) He thinks the rooms at the hotel cost too much.
(D) He is not going to stay at the hotel again.

Questions 156-157 refer to the following text message chain.

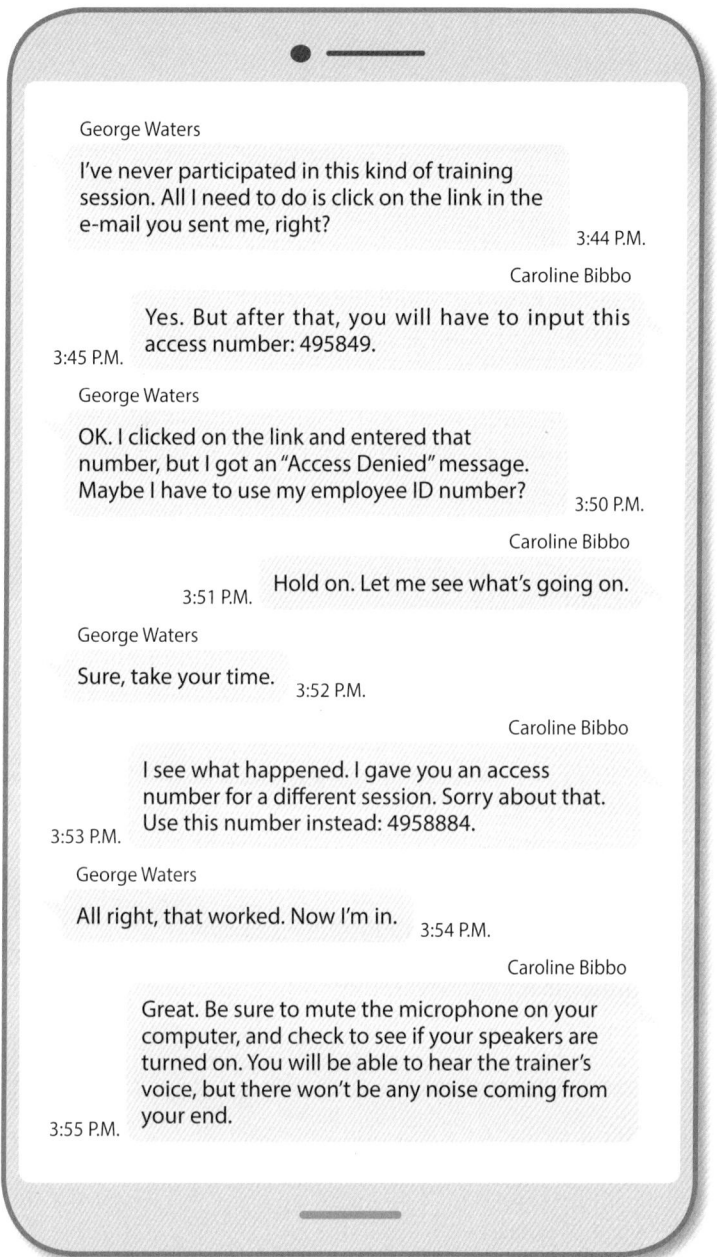

156. At 3:53 P.M., what does Ms. Bibbo most likely mean when she writes, "I see what happened"?

    (A) She is able to view a document now.
    (B) She is pointing out the man's mistake.
    (C) She discovered the reason for a problem.
    (D) She found the correct software update.

157. What is most likely true about Mr. Waters?

    (A) He will not say anything during his training session.
    (B) He frequently participates in video conferences.
    (C) He is going to lead a seminar.
    (D) He recently upgraded his computer system.

Questions 158-160 refer to the following memo.

From: Sid Pinkerton
To: All Staff
Date: 23 January
Subject: Paper waste

After careful review of our expenses from the previous year, we have decided to reduce operating costs by eliminating unnecessary waste. —[1]—. In particular, we believe we can save money by being smart when printing. I have noticed that many employees print simple documents, such as meeting summaries and draft proposals, on only one side. I understand that reading single-sided documents is more convenient than looking over double-sided ones, but this is a waste of paper. By not having to purchase paper as frequently, we will have extra money to spend in other areas, like company gatherings. —[2]—. I trust that all of you can make the proper call when printing something. If you have any questions, please talk to your manager. —[3]—. Single-sided printing should only be used when there is a very clear reason for doing so. —[4]—. Management appreciates your understanding in this matter.

158. What is a purpose of the memo?
(A) To discuss a budget issue
(B) To ask for input on a new project
(C) To request advice on a new policy
(D) To inform employees about upcoming repairs

159. According to the memo, what are staff urged to do?
(A) Print all client-related documents in color
(B) Notify maintenance of equipment problems
(C) Print basic materials on both sides of the paper
(D) Notify management of corporate purchases

160. In which of the positions marked [1], [2], [3], and [4] does the following sentence best belong?

"The notices we post on the wall of the staff lounge would be one example of this."

(A) [1]
(B) [2]
(C) [3]
(D) [4]

Questions 161-163 refer to the following article.

Parking Issue to be Addressed

A large number of Oaktown citizens have complained that the downtown area lacks parking spaces. —[1]—. Many of them have requested that the city council authorize the construction of a third parking lot to ease parking issues. —[2]—.

At its most recent meeting, the city council announced that it is going to conduct a survey to determine the causes of the parking problem. They will examine parking situations during various times on weekdays and weekends, and especially, during special events. —[3]—. When the survey is completed, the usage and availability of every parking spot in the city will be known.

"We know in general that parking problems are caused by the increase in visitors to small businesses in the area," said city manager Rachel Jenkins. —[4]—.

---

161. How many parking lots are currently in downtown Oaktown?

(A) One
(B) Two
(C) Three
(D) Four

162. What is indicated about the survey?

(A) It will determine parking demand at different times.
(B) It will be paid for by a private organization.
(C) It will involve volunteers from the city.
(D) It will focus only on parking issues on weekdays.

163. In which of the positions marked [1], [2], [3], and [4] does the following sentence best belong?

"However, we'll need to see specific numbers before we decide to build another lot."

(A) [1]
(B) [2]
(C) [3]
(D) [4]

GO ON TO THE NEXT PAGE

Questions 164-167 refer to the following Web page.

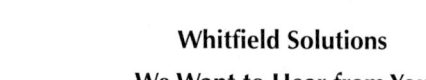

Whitfield Solutions
We Want to Hear from You

Whitfield Solutions has been in the polling business for more than half a century. Most of our competitors use internet polls to get their information. However, we believe in personally talking to every single respondent over the telephone. This allows us to receive comprehensive answers that other types of polls cannot provide. We also confirm that all of our respondents are legal adults, 18 years of age or older. To reduce the possibility of biased data, we randomly select the phone numbers of the people we call.

If you would like to see how people feel about various current issues and events, click on the "View Polls" icon on our Web page. We update our polls every week, and you can monitor how the results change from month to month. If you are interested in using any of our polls, you must first receive permission to do so. Go to the Contacts section of our site and click on the tab for our Legal Department. You will be directed to a page where you will be asked to complete a simple form that describes your reasons for using the data. We will send you a reply within one day of your application.

164. The word "comprehensive" in paragraph 1, line 4, is closest in meaning to

(A) absolute
(B) detailed
(C) understandable
(D) basic

165. What is NOT stated about poll participants?

(A) They are adults.
(B) They are contacted by telephone.
(C) They are paid for their services.
(D) They are chosen at random.

166. What is true about Whitfield Solutions?

(A) It operates in only one city.
(B) Its polls require money to access.
(C) Its Web site is updated weekly.
(D) It was founded two decades ago.

167. How can readers obtain permission to use polls?

(A) By speaking to a Whitfield employee
(B) By submitting information online
(C) By writing a letter
(D) By emailing a manager

Questions 168-171 refer to the following article.

Madrid Welcomes Business Guru

Madrid (12 July) – The Madrid Entrepreneurial Convention (MEC) proudly welcomes Emily Jimenez, founder of several well-known startup companies. The convention will take place in the Madrid Civic Center from 15 to 18 August. Entrepreneurs and visitors from all around Madrid are expected to attend. Organizers say that nearly 3,000 people have already registered for the event. As the keynote speaker for the event, Ms. Jimenez will share her experiences, which you can read about in more detail in her newly released book, *The Road to a Successful New Venture*. In her seminars, Ms. Jimenez always stresses the importance of careful and meticulous preparation when starting a new business. One of the crucial points Ms. Jimenez mentions in her book is that, "Marketing is key. You have to make advertisements that will immediately draw attention to your business. Sure, if you have a lot of money, you can keep trying again, but not many people have those kinds of financial resources."

Ms. Jimenez is currently working on a new project in London, where she has resided for nearly 20 years. "I grew up in Madrid," Ms. Jimenez said. "I agreed to speak at this convention because I wanted to come back to the place that made me who I am. There's so much opportunity here, and I want to show the participants that they can accomplish anything they want. This event can really help participants get focused on improving their businesses. I hope that they will learn from my experience."

Tickets for the convention can be reserved online for $150 or bought at the door for $170. For more information, go to the convention's Web site at www.mcc.es.org.

---

168. What is the article mainly discussing?

(A) The expansion of a retail chain
(B) The advantages of starting a new company
(C) A business expert's attendance at an event
(D) Advice on how to acquire financial donations

169. According to the article, what did Ms. Jimenez recently do?

(A) She published a book.
(B) She moved to London.
(C) She sold her store.
(D) She went on a radio show.

170. What does Mr. Jimenez say is an important factor for new business owners?

(A) Offering special discounts every month
(B) Designing a product that can be marketed to various age groups
(C) Creating ads that will quickly attract customers
(D) Entering partnerships with other businesses

171. Why did Ms. Jimenez decide to participate in the convention?

(A) To encourage entrepreneurs in her hometown
(B) To hire more qualified employees for her company
(C) To find better ways to promote her services
(D) To conduct research for her new project

GO ON TO THE NEXT PAGE

Questions 172-175 refer to the following online chat discussion.

Chris Hammond [8:40 A.M.]
I'm down here in the meeting room, and I can't seem to connect the laptop to the wall monitor. Can someone give me a hand?

Sierra Martinson [8:41 A.M.]
You should try restarting the laptop. That usually works for me when I have that problem.

Dianne Beauregard [8:43 A.M.]
I thought everything was supposed to be set up by 8:30 A.M. I'm a little worried because the new recruits are going to be showing up soon.

Chris Hammond [8:45 A.M.]
David Klingler was originally in charge of setting everything up, but his meeting with the clients has gone on longer than expected. That's why I'm trying to take care of it.

Chris Hammond [8:46 A.M.]
OK, it still doesn't work. Do you mind coming here, Sierra?

Sierra Martinson [8:46 A.M.]
Be there in a minute.

Dianne Beauregard [8:47 A.M.]
Is everything else prepared?

Chris Hammond [8:48 A.M.]
Yes, I made sure that the presentation was thoroughly reviewed by other team members. Also, I've printed all of the paperwork that the new recruits will complete.

Dianne Beauregard [8:51 A.M.]
Great. I'll drop by at 11:45 A.M. to accompany everyone to lunch. One of you needs to collect the completed forms, and then drop them off at the HR office so that Sylvia can start making the employee IDs.

Chris Hammond [8:57 A.M.]
I'll do that. By the way, Sierra just solved the problem. We're all set to begin now.

172. What is Mr. Hammond preparing to do?

(A) Demonstrate a new product
(B) Train some new workers
(C) Visit a client
(D) Print some paperwork

173. Why was the meeting room not set up by 8:30 A.M.?

(A) Because Mr. Klingler is out sick
(B) Because an access card did not work
(C) Because a meeting is running late
(D) Because a laptop could not be found

174. At 8:46 A.M., what does Ms. Martinson mean when he writes, "Be there in a minute"?

(A) She will receive a package.
(B) She is going to assist Mr. Hammond.
(C) She is going to greet some coworkers.
(D) She will bring a room key.

175. What will happen at 11:45 A.M.?

(A) Fingerprints will be taken.
(B) ID cards will be distributed.
(C) Ms. Beauregard will go to the meeting room.
(D) Mr. Hammond will give an introductory speech.

Questions 176-180 refer to the following e-mail and article.

To	lgreen@harringtonlibrary.org
From	jmoore@harringtonlibrary.org
Subject	Storage of new books
Date	February 27

Dear Lana,

In recent weeks, there have been some exciting events at the library. First, members of the Harrington Renovations Society have begun transforming a section of our fiction department into a multimedia center, free of charge to the library. Then, last week, the Youth Literacy Association donated around 700 children's books. Yesterday, we also managed to replace all our outdated encyclopedias using funds obtained from library events. Finally, we just heard from the National Organization for the Sight Impaired that they will be funding new purchases of 400 audio and large print books.

We obviously have inadequate shelving space to accommodate the recent acquisitions and donations. Therefore, I'd like to remove a number of books that are no longer in demand, but there is a lack of storage space to hold them. To solve this problem, one solution would be to hold our annual book sale quite a bit earlier than usual so that we can address this problem of housing all our books.

Could you please put this issue on the agenda for the March 7 Friends of the Harrington Library (FOHL) meeting? Although I will be on vacation from March 8 to March 15, feel free to contact me about developments in this matter.

Many thanks!
Jonathan Moore

Harrington (May 15) – Friends of Harrington Library (FOHL) held their annual sale on May 7. There were many bargains including books, CDs, and DVDs, selling for $2 on average. It was hugely successful, thanks in part to the large numbers of attendees at the Monique Street Spring Event. The sales record was $2,743, which is being used to buy four printers and two extra computers for the reference library and the multimedia center that opened April 12.

Until last year, the sale was held each September. However, as Lana Green, the library manager, explained, "We needed to get rid of so many books by March, so we decided to bring the date forward. Because we had so many things to sell, we decided to hold the annual sale in May. In May, many people congregate for the popular street event here."

"FOHL improves library service by holding this sale," commented head librarian Jonathan Moore. Proceeds from the sale have funded a variety of projects in past years, and this year, they allowed purchases large items such as computers and printers for the new multimedia center.

176. What did the Harrington Library buy in February?

(A) Encyclopedias
(B) Reading devices
(C) Dictionaries
(D) Children's books

177. Why did Mr. Moore recommend changing the date of the annual book sale?

(A) He thinks the change will draw more people.
(B) He will be on vacation on the originally scheduled date.
(C) The library needed extra storage space.
(D) The library is in need of more funds.

178. What is implied about the Harrington Library?

(A) It will soon relocate.
(B) It is supported by charitable organizations.
(C) It will be closed for the month of April.
(D) It holds a concert every June.

179. What will the money raised during the event be used towards?

(A) Buying new bookshelves
(B) Purchasing computers and printers
(C) Remodeling the children's book section
(D) Extending the library's nonfiction section

180. What is NOT mentioned about the multimedia center?

(A) It offers computer classes.
(B) The equipment is funded by book sales.
(C) A local group worked to improve it.
(D) It was set up in the fiction section.

Questions 181-185 refer to the following advertisement and e-mail.

Pine Tree Residence

Open Vacancy
Beautiful one- or two-bedroom apartments
State-of-the-art kitchens and large dining rooms

Exclusive offer for incoming residents
(signing a one-year lease is required)
One-bedroom unit: $1,500/month
Two-bedroom unit: $2,000/month
Includes heating and electricity costs
Tenants will have access to a convenient on-site laundry room
as well as a furnished recreation room and lounge.

40 Everglades Dr. Middleton, BA M4B 2E8
403-555-1042
www.pinetreeresidence.ca

To: Roger Kinley <rkinley@pinetree.com>
From: Lisa Heisburg <lheisburg@pinetree.com>
Subject: Update
Date: November 20
Attachment: Apartment_204A

Dear Mr. Kinley,

I drew up Christine Park's contract. She will be coming in this morning to finalize the one-year lease for Apartment 204A as well as bringing a check of $2,000 for the first month's rent. I will leave her completed paperwork and rent payment in your office this afternoon.

I will inform the maintenance department right away, so they can have this room ready by December 15. For your reference, I have attached a work order to this e-mail. As you'll see, Ms. Park decided on the living room with complementary coloring (color #3352, sky blue).

We only have two more vacant rooms. I have some appointments today to show the one-bedroom apartment, and I have a few appointments tomorrow to show the two-bedroom apartment. I anticipate both of them will have their leases signed before December. Afterwards, this building will be fully occupied.

Thank you.

Sincerely,

Lisa Heisburg

181. What is mentioned about the apartments for rent?

(A) They come fully furnished.
(B) They each have a dining area.
(C) They have recently been renovated.
(D) They are all equipped with an air conditioner.

182. What is suggested about Ms. Park?

(A) She will move into her apartment in November.
(B) She requested that a heater be repaired.
(C) She has renewed her lease for another year.
(D) She has chosen a two-bedroom apartment.

183. What does Ms. Heisburg say she will do?

(A) Give information to the maintenance staff
(B) Sign documents on behalf of Ms. Park
(C) Negotiate a price with a tenant
(D) Meet Mr. Kinley for an appointment

184. In the e-mail, the phrase "drew up" in paragraph 1, line 1, is closest in meaning to

(A) prepared
(B) illustrated
(C) removed
(D) attracted

185. According to the e-mail, what is suggested about the apartments at Pine Tree Residence?

(A) Their electricity costs will increase in December.
(B) They will all be rented soon.
(C) Their heating systems will be upgraded.
(D) They will all be painted blue.

GO ON TO THE NEXT PAGE

Questions 186-190 refer to the following credit card statement and e-mails.

Page 1

Name: Claude Reardon
Credit Card Number (Last Four Digits: 3833)

PURCHASES (Sept. 4 – Oct. 3)

Date	Business	Charge
Sept. 6	Nanna Bakery	$39.54
Sept. 8	New Style Clothes	$61.99
Sept. 12	Emerson Art Supplies	$46.00
Sept. 18	L.R. Nelson Outdoor Wear	$92.76
Sept. 21	Windsor Suits	$110.14
Sept. 27	Oceanside Apparel	$55.82
Oct. 2	Seascape Supermarket	$47.25

To	information@emersonartsupplies.com
From	creardon@privatemail.com
Subject	Purchase
Date	October 6

To Whom It May Concern,

Last month, I made a purchase at your store with my credit card, but I believe a mistake was made. I ordered a pastel set over the telephone and was charged $46.00 despite the fact that the set was on sale for $40.00. Even though you normally charge $10.00 for shipping, I took advantage of your special offer that stated that all customers who spent $30.00 or more received free shipping. Therefore, I would appreciate it if you would refund me the additional $6.00 I was overcharged.

Respectfully yours,

Claude Reardon

To: creardon@privatemail.com
From: information@emersonartsupplies.com
Subject: Re: Purchase
Date: October 7

Dear Mr. Reardon,

Emerson Art Supplies received your e-mail on October 6, and we promptly looked into the matter. According to the representative who took your order, you requested that the item be gift wrapped. Thus, the extra charge is actually the fee for this service. I apologize for any misunderstanding related to this. The representative should have made sure to mention this when explaining the final amount. As an apology for this, I would like to give you a choice of a $5.00 credit on this purchase or a $10.00 discount on a future purchase (minimum purchase amount of $60.00). Simply reply to this e-mail to let me know which one you prefer. We at Emerson Art Supplies look forward to serving your needs in the future.

Sincerely,

Martha White
Customer Service Manager

186. What did Mr. Reardon use his credit card for the most in September?

(A) Travel
(B) Clothing
(C) Dining
(D) Stationery

187. When did Mr. Reardon speak to a company representative on the phone?

(A) On September 6
(B) On September 12
(C) On September 21
(D) On September 27

188. In the second e-mail, the word "promptly" in line 1 is closest in meaning to

(A) completely
(B) immediately
(C) apparently
(D) skillfully

189. How much did the gift wrapping service cost?

(A) $5.00
(B) $6.00
(C) $10.00
(D) $20.00

190. What did Ms. White ask Mr. Reardon to do?

(A) Select his preferred form of compensation
(B) Confirm his delivery address
(C) Rate the quality of the item
(D) Complete a customer satisfaction survey

GO ON TO THE NEXT PAGE

Questions 191-195 refer to the following e-mail, brochure, and text message.

From	damatto@highcrossings.co.uk
To	romano@venturihotel.co.it
Date	February 7
Subject	Hiking group services

Hello Ms. Romano,

I represent High Crossings, an outdoor adventure tour group that runs programs all around Europe. We plan to lead hikes around Val Alba Reserve and are interested in using the Venturi Hotel as a base of operations because it's quite close to the reserve. If you could, I would like you to send me the following details:

- Your vacancy during the month of June
- The menu options for your morning and evening meals
- Resources for area trails and hiking recommendations
- Public transportation within the city and shuttle services to and from the airport

We plan to have a group of 10 to 15 people and are interested in any group discounts that you may offer. From what is listed on your Web site, I'm sure that we will be able to reach a compromise on pricing.

I look forward to hearing from you.

Best regards,

Chris d'Amatto
Tour Organizer
High Crossings

Trek through the Alps

It's our pleasure to announce the latest High Crossings European outing in the Italian Alps to our already long list of adventure tourism packages. Experience the incredible Italian mountain reserve of Val Alba, from June 11 to 15. This wilderness, northeast of Venice, has towering peaks and deep, forested valleys.

Our tour package will include four nights and five days at the comfortable Silverleaf Resort, which will also provide our daily meals, bus rides to the trails, and transportation to and from the airport.

Book our packages before April 30 for a discount:
Basic room: $750 (1 bed, 1 bath)
Deluxe room: $1,000 (2 beds, 1 bath)
Grand room: $1,200 (suitable for a family of four)
Executive room: $1,550 (suitable for groups of five to seven, easy access to the parking lot)

The trip in June is limited to just 15 hikers, and prices go up in May, so act now! Visit www.highcrossings.co.uk or email reservations@highcrossings.co.uk for additional information, including maps and menus, and booking services.

From: Jamie Aure
Sent: 1:03 P.M., April 12

Good afternoon. I just got a call from Mr. d'Amatto saying that he has a deluxe room remaining, which I went ahead and booked. Also, the room has a futon, which means that all three of us will have a place to sleep without having to upgrade to the grand room. I'm really looking forward to this vacation!

191. According to the e-mail, what does Mr. d'Amatto want to negotiate?

(A) The transportation to the reserve
(B) The tour guide wages
(C) The accommodation fees
(D) The meals being served

192. According to the brochure, what is High Crossings now offering?

(A) An opportunity to extend a trip
(B) An on-site translator
(C) A new destination
(D) A tour of historic sites

193. What is suggested about the Venturi Hotel?

(A) It will not be reserved by Mr. d'Amatto.
(B) It has excellent reviews on its Web site.
(C) It does not offer a complimentary breakfast.
(D) It is situated inside of the Val Alba Reserve.

194. How much will Ms. Aure pay for her tour package?

(A) $750
(B) $1,000
(C) $1,200
(D) $1,550

195. Why did Ms. Aure send the text message?

(A) To make sure a certain service is included
(B) To change the dates of a vacation
(C) To request a room upgrade
(D) To provide information about a booking

GO ON TO THE NEXT PAGE

Questions 196-200 refer to the following e-mail, letter, and calendar.

From	jackiep@egorilla.net
To	bernardc@egorilla.net
Subject	Company credit card
Date	21 June

Dear Mr. Collier,

Your application for the company credit card has been received. To complete the process, you must submit one of the following documents:
- A schedule indicating more than two international business trips within the calendar year
- Budget report showing expected business-related expenses of over $500
- Confirmation signed by your direct supervisor stating that your job duties will include entertainment of corporate clients

As we finalize your request, please visit the company Web site to look over our travel and expense policies. Here are some key points to note:
- The company will cover any meals, provided they do not go over the daily allotted amount.
- A manager must preapprove use of a rental vehicle before you submit a request to corporate travel management.
- All accommodations and transportation costs must be approved by corporate travel management.

Warmest regards,

Jackie Philman
Corporate Travel Management, Electronic Gorilla

The Global Technology Forum (GTF)
Bernard Collier
Electronic Gorilla
2195 Wolf Pen Road
San Francisco, CA 94107

Dear Mr. Collier,

Thank you for registering for this year's GTF in Singapore. We have received your payment of $550. We look forward to your attendance.

We have assembled a great lineup of speakers and discussion panelists for this year's event. We are expecting a larger turnout than in past years, so sign up quickly. Visit our Web site to register for the talks you would like to attend. Event organizers will also be hosting a continuing education seminar this year exclusively for GTF members. Throughout the week, there will be plenty of social gatherings to help you network. Snacks and beverages will be provided throughout the event, but attendees will be responsible for their own meals.

For all inquiries, please send an e-mail to help@gtf.org.

Best,

GTF Representative

Itinerary for Bernard Collier: April 5 – 10

April 5-6
7:30 A.M. Depart from Seattle, WA (Flight UB14)
2:00 P.M. (April 6) Land in Singapore
3:00 P.M. Check in at Grandfall Hotel (arrive via airport shuttle)

April 7
10:00 A.M. – 11:00 A.M. Introductory Speaker
11:30 A.M. – 6:00 P.M. Speaking Panels
7:00 P.M. – 9:00 P.M. Networking Event

April 8
10:00 A.M. – 5:00 P.M. Industry Speakers
6:00 P.M. – 9:00 P.M. Continuing Education Seminar

April 9
10:00 A.M. – 4:00 P.M. Discussion Groups
5:00 P.M. – 9:00 P.M. Award Ceremony and Keynote Speaker

April 10
12:00 P.M. Arrive at Airport (via hotel shuttle)
2:35 P.M. Depart Singapore (Flight UB33)
4:15 P.M. (April 9) Land in Seattle

---

196. What qualifies Mr. Collier to receive a company credit card?

(A) He will take some clients out for dinner.
(B) He will be out of the country for more than two days.
(C) He recently booked an international flight.
(D) He paid a registration fee that was over $500.

197. What is the purpose of the letter?

(A) To verify a payment
(B) To discuss a schedule change
(C) To check a food preference
(D) To arrange transportation

198. In the letter, the word "assembled" in paragraph 2, line 1, is closest in meaning to

(A) manufactured
(B) installed
(C) gathered
(D) connected

199. What is suggested about Mr. Collier?

(A) He is organizing a social gathering.
(B) He is going to receive an award.
(C) He will give a keynote speech.
(D) He has a GTF membership.

200. What expense policy does NOT apply to Mr. Collier?

(A) The policy on hotel accommodations
(B) The policy on vehicle rentals
(C) The policy on meal expenses
(D) The policy on flight reservations

Stop! This is the end of the test. If you finish before time is called, you may go back to Part 5, 6, and 7 and check your work.

NO TEST MATERIAL ON THIS PAGE

NO TEST MATERIAL ON THIS PAGE

Answer Keys

MP3, 해석, 해설 온라인 무료 제공
모바일: QR코드 스캔을 통해 MP3 음원 바로 듣기 / 정답, 해석, 해설 바로 보기
PC: 파고다북스 사이트(www.pagodabook.com) 접속 / 로그인 후 다운로드

Listening Comprehension

1 (B)	2 (B)	3 (A)	4 (C)	5 (C)	
6 (B)	7 (B)	8 (A)	9 (C)	10 (C)	
11 (C)	12 (C)	13 (A)	14 (C)	15 (A)	
16 (B)	17 (A)	18 (C)	19 (B)	20 (B)	
21 (A)	22 (B)	23 (B)	24 (C)	25 (A)	
26 (B)	27 (C)	28 (A)	29 (C)	30 (B)	
31 (A)	32 (A)	33 (D)	34 (C)	35 (B)	
36 (C)	37 (D)	38 (D)	39 (A)	40 (B)	
41 (C)	42 (B)	43 (C)	44 (A)	45 (D)	
46 (D)	47 (B)	48 (A)	49 (B)	50 (C)	
51 (D)	52 (B)	53 (A)	54 (C)	55 (C)	
56 (D)	57 (A)	58 (A)	59 (A)	60 (A)	
61 (D)	62 (D)	63 (D)	64 (C)	65 (C)	
66 (D)	67 (C)	68 (C)	69 (D)	70 (B)	
71 (A)	72 (A)	73 (C)	74 (D)	75 (D)	
76 (B)	77 (D)	78 (A)	79 (B)	80 (B)	
81 (B)	82 (C)	83 (D)	84 (A)	85 (B)	
86 (D)	87 (A)	88 (D)	89 (C)	90 (B)	
91 (A)	92 (A)	93 (B)	94 (B)	95 (B)	
96 (C)	97 (A)	98 (D)	99 (A)	100 (D)	

Reading Comprehension

101 (A)	102 (B)	103 (B)	104 (A)	105 (C)
106 (C)	107 (D)	108 (D)	109 (B)	110 (C)
111 (D)	112 (D)	113 (C)	114 (D)	115 (A)
116 (D)	117 (B)	118 (C)	119 (B)	120 (D)
121 (D)	122 (C)	123 (D)	124 (A)	125 (B)
126 (C)	127 (A)	128 (B)	129 (B)	130 (D)
131 (B)	132 (A)	133 (A)	134 (B)	135 (C)
136 (B)	137 (A)	138 (C)	139 (B)	140 (D)
141 (B)	142 (C)	143 (B)	144 (A)	145 (D)
146 (B)	147 (B)	148 (B)	149 (A)	150 (B)
151 (A)	152 (C)	153 (A)	154 (D)	155 (B)
156 (C)	157 (A)	158 (A)	159 (C)	160 (D)
161 (B)	162 (A)	163 (D)	164 (B)	165 (C)
166 (C)	167 (B)	168 (C)	169 (A)	170 (C)
171 (A)	172 (B)	173 (C)	174 (B)	175 (C)
176 (A)	177 (C)	178 (B)	179 (B)	180 (A)
181 (B)	182 (D)	183 (A)	184 (A)	185 (B)
186 (B)	187 (B)	188 (B)	189 (B)	190 (A)
191 (C)	192 (C)	193 (A)	194 (B)	195 (D)
196 (D)	197 (A)	198 (C)	199 (D)	200 (B)

파고다토익
시험 직전
마무리 TEST 3
모의고사

초판 1쇄 인쇄 2017년 12월 27일
초판 1쇄 발행 2018년 1월 2일
초판 16쇄 발행 2024년 9월 30일

지 은 이 | 파고다교육그룹 언어교육연구소
펴 낸 이 | 박경실
펴 낸 곳 | **PAGODA Books** 파고다북스
출판등록 | 2005년 5월 27일 제 300-2005-90호
주   소 | 06614 서울특별시 서초구 강남대로 419, 19층(서초동, 파고다타워)
전   화 | (02) 6940-4070
팩   스 | (02) 536-0660
홈페이지 | www.pagodabook.com

저작권자 | ⓒ 2018 파고다아카데미

이 책의 저작권은 저자와 출판사에 있습니다. 서면에 의한 저작권자와 출판사의 허락 없이
내용의 일부 혹은 전부를 인용 및 복제하거나 발췌하는 것을 금합니다.

Copyright ⓒ 2018 by PAGODA Academy

All rights reserved. No part of this publication may be reproduced, stored
in a retrieval system, or transmitted, in any form, or by any means, electronic,
mechanical, photocopying, recording or otherwise, without the prior written
permission of the copyright holder and the publisher.

ISBN 978-89-6281-808-6 (13740)

파고다북스	www.pagodabook.com
파고다 어학원	www.pagoda21.com
파고다 인강	www.pagodastar.com
테스트 클리닉	www.testclinic.com

| 낙장 및 파본은 구매처에서 교환해 드립니다.

PAGODA Books

DATA SHEET

PAGODA Books

※ 본 OMR 카드는 실전 연습용으로 제공되었으며, OMR 성적 처리는 별도로 제공되지 않음을 알려드립니다.

ANSWER SHEET

PAGODA Books

문제번호

성명

LISTENING COMPREHENSION (Part I~IV)

READING COMPREHENSION (Part V~VII)

DATA SHEET

PAGODA Books

※ 본 OMR 카드는 실전 연습용으로 제공되었으며, OMR 성적 처리는 별도로 제공되지 않음을 알려드립니다.

ANSWER SHEET

PAGODA Books

문제번호

성명

LISTENING COMPREHENSION (Part I ~ IV)

READING COMPREHENSION (Part V ~ VII)

DATA SHEET

PAGODA Books

※ 본 OMR 카드는 실전 연습용으로 제공되었으며, OMR 성적 처리는 별도로 제공되지 않음을 알려드립니다.

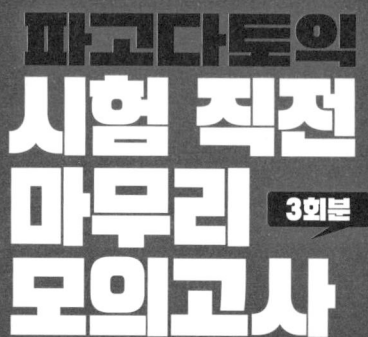

파고다토익
시험 직전
마무리 모의고사 3회분

유형, 난이도, 구성
정기 토익과 100% 똑같다!

❶ 시험 직전 꼭 풀어야 할 문제만 골라 3회분 모의고사로 구성!
최신 정기 토익 출제 경향을 완벽 분석, 반영한 600제 수록

❷ MP3, 정답, 해석, 해설 온라인 무료 제공!
모바일 : QR코드 스캔을 통해 MP3 음원 바로 듣기 / 정답, 해석, 해설 바로 보기
PC : 파고다북스 사이트 접속 / 로그인 후 다운로드

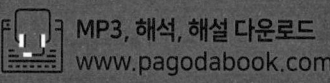

MP3, 해석, 해설 다운로드
www.pagodabook.com

PRINTED WITH SOY INK

ECO LIFE WITH PAGODA
친환경 소재인 콩기름 잉크로 인쇄.

입문 · 초급 · 중급 · 고급 · **실전**

PAGODA Books
교재문의 02)6940-4070

9 788962 818086
ISBN 978-89-6281-808-6
13740

정 가 ₩ 9,900